Programmed Learning Aid for

THE CONSTITUTION OF THE UNITED STATES

Programmed Learning Aid for

THE CONSTITUTION OF THE UNITED STATES

JOSEPH T. KEENAN
De Paul University

Coordinating Editor
ROGER H. HERMANSON
Georgia State University

LEARNING SYSTEMS COMPANY

A division of
RICHARD D. IRWIN, INC.   Homewood, Illinois   60430

Also available through
IRWIN-DORSEY INTERNATIONAL   London, England   WC2H 9NJ
IRWIN-DORSEY LIMITED   Georgetown, Ontario   L7G 4B3

To James Madison, John Marshall and Kitty Keenan.
(*Not necessarily in that order, dear.*)

ISBN 0-256-01615-1
Printed in the United States of America

1 2 3 4 5 6 7 8 9 0 K 4 3 2 1 0 9 8 7 6 5

FOREWORD

Each of the books comprising the Programmed Learning Aid Series is in programmed learning format to provide the reader with a quick, efficient, and effective means of grasping the essential subject matter.

The specific benefits of the programmed method of presentation are as follows:

1. It keeps the reader *active* in the learning process and increases comprehension level.
2. Incorrect responses are *corrected immediately*.
3. Correct responses are *reinforced immediately*.
4. The method is *flexible*. Those who need more "tutoring" receive it because they are encouraged to reread frames in which they have missed any of the questions asked.
5. The method makes learning seem like a game.

The method of programming used in this PLAID on *The Constitution of the United States* and in most of the other PLAIDs is unique and simple to use. Begin by reading Frame 1^1 in Chapter 1. At the end of that frame answer the True-False questions given. To determine the correctness of responses, merely turn the page and examine the answers given in Answer Frame 1^1. The reader is told *why* each statement is true or false. Performance on the questions given is used as a measure of understanding of all the materials in Frame 1^1. If any of the questions are missed, reread Frame 1^1 before continuing on to Frame 2^1. This same procedure should be used throughout the book. Specific instructions are given throughout as to where to turn next to continue working the program.

The reader may desire to go through the PLAID a second time leaving out the programming questions and answers, or may desire to further test understanding by going through it a second time answering all of the questions once again and rereading only those frames in which comprehension is unsatisfactory.

PLAIDs are continuously updated in new printings to provide the reader with the latest subject content in the field.

Roger H. Hermanson
Coordinating Editor and Programmer

PREFACE

At 8:30 P.M. (EDT) on August 8, 1974, he met privately with a group of faithful Congressional supporters.

"I just hope I didn't let you down," he said, and suddenly the repressed emotions of many months erupted. The president of the United States broke down in tears.

Half an hour later a remarkably composed Richard Nixon, facing a battery of lights and cameras, announced his resignation to the American people because "it has become evident to me that I no longer have a strong enough political base in the Congress" and because "America needs a full-time President" (not one who must devote time to defending himself).

There was no apology, no bitterness, no vindictiveness, no self-pity. The president went out with chin up and with all the dignity he could summon. Perhaps nothing in his entire presidency ever became Richard Nixon quite so much as the leaving of it.

At 11:35 the following day, in accordance with provisions of the Presidential Succession Act of March 1, 1972, Presidential Aide Gen. Alexander M. Haig, Jr. delivered the following message to the Secretary of State:

> The White House
> Washington

> Aug. 9, 1974

> Dear Mr. Secretary:
> I hereby resign the office of President of the United States.

> Sincerely,

> Richard Nixon

> (to)
> The Honorable Henry A. Kissinger
> The Secretary of State
> Washington, D.C. 20520

At noon, Gerald R. Ford was sworn in as president of the United States. For the first time in history, the wealthiest and most productive nation in the world would be directed by a nonelected vice president who had succeeded to the presidency. Before the month was up another nonelected vice president—Nelson Rockefeller—would be appointed by the nonelected president.

It had been a week of jeers and cheers, of signs proclaiming "Hail to the Chief" and "Jail to the Chief," "Good luck" and "Good riddance"—a week in which the office that had challenged the talents of Washington, Jefferson, Lincoln, and the Roosevelts had been indelibly disgraced. The rest of the world, kept abreast by the press and satellite television, "attended" the wake for the American Presidency.

But when the full impact of what had taken place began to register, the expressions of condolences were canceled out by reactions of wonderment and admiration. For nobody had been killed. No shots had been fired, no blood spilled, no soldiers called up. No insurrectionist junta challenged the new regime. Even the Democrats applauded, sent wishes of good luck, and promised to cooperate. The only reported injury was to one of the movers who bruised a toe when he dropped one of Pat Nixon's suitcases.

The presidency's darkest hour was also Democracy's brightest moment. A musty, dusty document known as the American Constitution had become a living, pulsing instrument of government that stretched and breathed and accommodated and changed its mind and served as a master plan that directed the daily lives of 200 million people.

The burglar tools which opened the doors of Democratic headquarters at Watergate had opened a renaissance of interest in the Constitution. Radio and television talk shows discussed the document at great length; the intent of the Founding Fathers and the impact of Supreme Court decisions became "in" topics at the smartest dinner conversations; many colleges reported increased interest in political science courses; at high school and junior high levels, students discussed impeachment and *United States* v *Nixon* and learned that s-u-b-p-o-e-n-a can also be spelled s-u-b-p-e-n-a.

I hope that this slender volume will suit the needs of all who seek to become better acquainted with the U.S. Constitution. The built-in programming, the glossary, the sample examinations, and the story of the development of the Constitution from conception through ratification are all designed for easy reading and comprehension. Most of all I hope we have captured some small spark of the spirit that motivated the Founding Fathers and makes this governmental blueprint one of the most fascinating and important documents in the history of world civilization.

Pages of "thank yous" must be compressed into a paragraph. It was Bill Crawford's (President of Learning Systems) idea all the way; his gentle prodding and expert needling, his encouragement and, most of all, his enthusiasm, moved the manuscript from conception to press. His secretary, Marlene Maxon, cheerfully handled reams of correspondence and dozens of telephoned corrections. Shamelessly, I took advantage of the research expertise of Douglas Kmiec, a brilliant law student at U.S.C.; of the combined wisdom of Robert Weclew and Harry Thomson, professors of Law and Political Science, respectively, at De Paul University; and of Kendall Byrnes, professor of Law at John Marshall University, who also read the manuscript critically. At the top of my "bibliography" is Ralph Mailliard, retired professor of History at De Paul and the closest approximation to a walking encyclopedia of American History I have ever known. And then there was six-year-old Christopher who, although he practiced with crayon and left-handed scissors on a few sheets of immortal prose, will probably never realize how effectively he has rejuvenated his father's own constitutional process.

JOSEPH T. KEENAN
De Paul University

CONTENTS

chapter 1

WHY A CONSTITUTION?

Frame 1[1]

It was as though a group of carpenters had been called upon to add a dormer, a recreation room, and a back porch and then, without permission of the owner, decided to tear down the house and build a new one from scratch.

The little group of Founding Fathers, who first met in Philadelphia at the Constitutional Convention in May 1787 had gathered, according to specific instructions, "for the sole and express purpose of revising the Articles of Confederation" and of making recommendations to the Congress that would "render the federal constitution adequate to the exigencies of government and the preservation of the union." Clearly, their powers were advisory.

But in the very first week the idea was broached of tearing up the old constitution and blueprinting a completely new one. A plan for a new constitution was proposed and in a brazen breech of authority the Convention voted to consider this plan in all its details before it would consider any other business. The struggle for acceptance of a new instrument of government, waged by 55 Founding Fathers in heavy worsted suits, continued throughout the steamy summer of 1787; the campaign for ratification dragged on for another ten months. It is no idle metaphor to say that the United States Constitution is a child of chance, conceived illegitimately, and brought into the world unwanted by many members of its own family.

This book, programmed for easy understanding, tells that story of conception, birth, and growth of what is now the world's oldest *written* Constitution—and its most successful.

The Articles of Confederation

From 1781 through 1788 our country operated under a written constitution known as the Articles of Confederation. Adopted during the Revolutionary War, the Articles were inadequate for several reasons: there was no chief executive, no power of taxation, no provision for regulation of commerce, and no federal judiciary.

Lacking both armed might and international respect, American ships suffered piracy and insult on the high seas. At home, with no intelligent centrally-enforced tariff policy, manufacturers were in danger of being wiped out by cheap imports. Spaniard, Englishman, and Indian menaced points along frontiers defended only by local vigilante groups or pussycat state militias. Thirteen separate sets of state laws occasionally created frustrating, bewildering, and sometimes comical legal situations.

Among those who blushed in embarrassment was John Adams, minister to England, who is said to have broached the subject of a commercial treaty to a member of the Foreign Office.

"Would you like one treaty or thirteen, Mr. Adams?" asked the British diplomat.

Although complications were compounded in multiples of 13, people can endure many hardships in normal times. But unrest intensified when an economic recession, triggered by a money crisis, struck at parts of the country about 1785. Usually, this ferment was merely reflected in belt-tightening, in indignant letters-to-the-editor, and in increased gripes. In New Hampshire, however, the governor was forced to call

1

out the militia to disperse a mob that had gathered at the state capitol in an effort to force the state to issue more paper money.

While the New Hampshire incident was swiftly squelched, the ineptitude of the Articles was dramatized by a more serious incident in Massachusetts known in history as Shays' Rebellion.

Shays' Rebellion

Thirty-nine year old Daniel Shays, who participated in the Battle of Bunker Hill and rose to the rank of captain in the War of Independence, was reasonably typical of hundreds of returning veterans who lived on farms in western Massachusetts. Disillusioned because he had to wait for his back pay, caught between the hard-money squeeze and the state's demand for extortionate land taxes payable in specie (coin), Shays looked to the state for relief. But there was no one to whom he could even protest, for many of the districts of western Massachusetts were without effective representation in the As-

sembly in Boston because the districts were either too poor to send representatives or because the men who would best represent them could not meet the legislative property qualifications. The merchant and seafaring members of the Boston Assembly ignored the pleas of the western farmers and adjourned in July 1786.

Shut out at the state house, the western farmers called unofficial county conventions to talk things over and put the torch to the fires of discontent. Quickly, their disenchantment was translated into action. They attacked and closed several civil courts where foreclosure proceedings were taking away scores of farms. When ringleaders were arrested and charged with inciting riots, the furious farmers proceeded to shut down the criminal courts.

This was too much for Governor Bowdoin who in January 1787, called the militia to put down the rebel cause, which by this time was headed by Shays. Sporadically, the fighting continued for more than a month before Shays' pathetic "army" of perhaps 1,200 men was routed.

Indicate whether each of the following statements is true or false by writing "T" or "F" in the space provided.

_____ 1. The Founding Fathers were given instructions to meet in Philadelphia to construct a completely new constitution for the nation.

_____ 2. The Constitution was complete and ready for ratification in late 1776.

_____ 3. The Articles of Confederation were clearly inadequate.

_____ 4. Shays' Rebellion was carried out by an "army" of western Massachusetts farmers and was directed against the courts.

Now turn to Answer frame 1[1] on page 4 and check your responses.

Frame 2[1]

Why the Articles were weak

It was no mere accident or constitutional oversight that the Articles of Confederation stressed the principles of state sovereignty and a weak central authority. The men who drew up the Articles and the citizens of the states which ratified them clearly wanted them precisely that way.

State sovereignty was a cherished and jeal-

ously guarded prerogative—one of those rights for which the colonists were fighting and dying at the time the Articles were adopted, one of the ideals which had prompted their forefathers to risk the hazardous journey to the new land. Many speakers accurately predicted the perils of a federated system hobbled by a jellyfish central authority. But implanted in the mind and heritage of every colonist was a congenital distrust of the strong executive (king), his central court system, his calloused tax collector, and his military collaborators.

But after six years of rule under the Articles, it was generally recognized that a few "adjustments" were in order. Few of the members of the unicameral Congress realized that in calling for a Constitutional Convention to consider these "adjustments," they were voting for their own dismissal.

Historical precedents

Precedents for the *written* American Constitution were almost nonexistent in continental European history or in the English governmental system, but the idea was well established in the organizational structure of the English Puritan Church of the 17th century. The Constitution of 1789 was also foreshadowed by an instance in 17th century American colonial government, in American state governments of the late 1770s and early 1780s and, of course, in the Articles of Confederation. The Founding Fathers must have also found great philosophical encouragement in the works of certain early Romantic poets, writers, and artists as well as in the political treatises of several visionary writers prominent in the 18th century movement, primarily European, known as the Enlightenment.

The English to this day have no written Constitution. Their structure of government and cherished rights are rooted in custom, tradition, the common law, Acts of Parliament, judicial interpretations, and in several noteworthy documents, some of which were executed at point of sword as well as pen.

The Great Charter (Magna Carta) of 1215, cornerstone of English political freedom, was primarily an agreement between king and barons to live up to the terms of their feudal contract. It came about, not out of love or trust or humanitarian impulse, but because of widespread fear, suspicion, and downright distrust for King John, whose name is etched in history as one of England's most important monarchs only because he was also one of the most deceitful and incompetent and unscrupulous.

The historic Petition of Right (1629) likewise was forced down the throat of an unfortunate king. The king was Charles I, who 20 years later was to suffer a separation of his head from his shoulders at the hands of rebellious subjects. When Charles affixed his signature to the Petition of Right he in effect acknowledged that he had been acting unconstitutionally. It was a truly landmark event in English constitutional history, guaranteeing citizens freedom from arrest without cause, from enforced quartering of His Majesty's soldiers, from military law in time of peace, and from taxation without consent of Parliament. The fact that Charles sometimes abrogated the Petition of Right, just as some kings rejected the Magna Carta, did not dim the lustre of the glorious day.

England's only noteworthy attempt at government under a written constitution began in 1653 when Puritan leaders formed a Protectorate under a document known as the Instrument of Government. *Among the nations of the world the Instrument of Government was the first written constitution of the modern type. It may be recognized as a reasonable prototype of the American Constitution of 1789.*

The executive power was wielded by a Lord Protector, Oliver Cromwell, subject to the advice of a Council of State. Legislative authority was vested in a Parliament apportioned somewhat imperfectly according to population. The Lord Protector's legislative veto could be overridden by a simple majority of the 460 member Parliament, 30 of whom were from Ireland and 30 from Scotland. Catholics and Royalists in the recent Civil War were disfranchised, and religious freedom was granted to all except Catholics and Episcopalians.

Established by military men, the Instrument of Government almost immediately degenerated into a harsh military rule. It could not have been more unpopular in papist-hating England if it had called for His Holiness and his cardinals to cross the channel and rule by proclamation from the pulpit of Canterbury. Within three years the "Instrument" was scuttled and succeeded by a new constitution, the Humble Petition and Advice, equally inefficient, unpopular, and inconsequential. Oliver Cromwell changed worlds in 1658 and two years later the Stuart monarch, Parliament, and the Anglican Church returned to power in Restoration England.

The new king was the handsome and irre-

Answer frame 1[1]

1. False. They had been instructed to gather "for the sole and express purpose of revising the Articles of Confederation" and making recommendations to the Congress as to the necessary changes. Their assigned role was merely advisory. They assumed for themselves the role of devising an entirely new constitution.

2. False. The correct year was 1787. The country operated under a written constitution known as the Articles of Confederation from 1781 through 1788. (The Declaration of Independence was signed in 1776.)

3. True. Under the Articles there was no chief executive, no power of taxation, no provision for regulation of commerce, and no federal judiciary. American ships suffered piracy, and manufacturers were damaged by cheap imports. The borders were threatened. Also, there was economic recession and violence.

4. True. The group attacked and closed several civil courts where foreclosure proceedings were taking place. After arrests were made they shut down the criminal courts. They were finally routed by the militia.

An attempt has been made in each frame throughout the PLAID to test the most important concepts within that frame. It is unlikely that this has been accomplished in every instance. Therefore, you should use your performance on the questions at the end of each frame as an indication of your comprehension of all of the concepts in that frame. If you missed any of the above, you should restudy Frame 1[1] before turning to Frame 2[1] on page 2. You should use this same procedure throughout the PLAID.

Frame 2[1] continued

sponsible Charles II, son of the beheaded Charles I, ablest and laziest of the Stuart line. When Charles II, the "merry monarch," agreed to the Restoration Settlement, he implied subtly but unmistakably that the king henceforth would be subject to limitations of power.

The historic English Bill of Rights, approved by William and Mary at the time of the Glorious Revolution, 1688, can be looked upon as a forerunner to the American Bill of Rights (the first ten amendments).

Government by compact

If the historical precedent for a written constitution is not to be found fully in the English governmental system, the principle of a written "compact" or agreement among people on how they were to be governed is clearly ingrained in Calvinist church organizational theory. (In America the Dutch and German Reform Churches and all Presbyterian branches were offshoots of Calvinism.)

In his *Institutes of the Christian Religion*, blueprint of Calvinist doctrine, John Calvin acknowledged that the church cannot even come into being except by common consent.

By far the best known of the many little "compact" forms of government in the American colonies had its origin in the cabin of the *Mayflower*. Shortly before landing on Plymouth Rock in November 1620, the men of the ship "solemnly and mutually in the presence of God and of one another," wrote out the Mayflower Compact by which they agreed to "covenant and combine ourselves together into a civil body politic."

This principle of government by written agreement was accepted 16 years later by Roger Williams and his tiny group of rebels who left Massachusetts for Providence, Rhode Island. Several other Rhode Island towns followed suit.

Indicate whether each of the following statements is true or false.

_____ 1. The Articles of Confederation were purposely designed to result in a weak "federal" government.

_____ 2. The United States Constitution was patterned after the English written constitution which is still in effect.

_____ 3. The Humble Petition and Advice Constitution of the English was the forerunner to the American Bill of Rights (which is comprised of the first ten amendments to the United States Constitution).

_____ 4. The Mayflower Compact was an agreement among the men of the ship on how they were to be governed.

Now turn to Answer frame 2¹ on page 6 and check your responses.

Frame 3¹

Fundamental Orders of Connecticut

In 1639 the colonists of Windsor, Wethersfield, and Hartford, Connecticut, consented to be ruled under a written constitution. The document specified that the freemen would gather annually in an election court to choose a governor and a board of magistrates. Each town would have four representatives at a general court which would also be attended by the governor and magistrates. The general court clearly dominated the governor.

The document became known as the Fundamental Orders of Connecticut and is generally considered to be the first modern written constitution, predating the English Instrument of Government by 14 years.

One common denominator lurks behind the Instrument of Government, the Mayflower Compact, the Compact executed by Roger Williams in Rhode Island, and the Fundamental Orders of Connecticut: all were illegal. The men who set up the Instrument of Government were constitutional imposters; the Mayflower Pilgrims realized they were landing on forbidden ground, for their grant of land was in Virginia; Roger Williams, banished from Massachusetts Bay, did not receive a legal charter for Providence until 1644, eight years after his Compact was executed, and the Connecticut River planters had neither title nor patent to their territory. History may never know for sure whether all four of these early constitutional experiments were merely special conscious efforts to justify illegal actions.

State constitutions

In the first five years of the American Revolution 11 states graphically crowned their declared breakaway from George III by establishing constitutions. Only Rhode Island and Connecticut, satisfied with their charters, did not adopt new constitutions.

Brevity was a common characteristic of these documents. Generally only the skeletal bones were provided, and the legislatures were empowered to pack in the flesh.

Another universal feature reflected the colonists' fear of the governor. Even though he no longer would be a representative of the king or the proprietor, the governor was in most cases carefully reduced in power at the expense of the legislature.

Seven of the 11 constitutions contained Bills of Rights, reflecting concern for some of the basic freedoms for which the colonists were fighting at the time.

The Articles of Confederation, which became effective on March 1, 1781, was the direct forerunner of the American Constitution. Under the Articles a Congress was established as the single agency of government and each state, though it might send from two to seven delegates, had *one vote*, regardless of size. Thus, little New Hampshire exerted the same influence as populous Virginia; Rhode Island was politically as powerful as Pennsylvania.

European states watched—and copied—the successful experiment on the other side of the Atlantic. The French overthrew two centuries

Answer frame 2¹

1. True. Many of the new settlers still feared central authority because of their past rule by European kings. State sovereignty is something they were fighting and dying for during the War of Independence at the time the Articles were written.
2. False. The English do not operate under a written constitution. However, many of the features of the United States Constitution were somewhat similar to those contained in the Instrument of Government under which the English operated for about three years.
3. False. The historic English Bill of Rights approved by William and Mary at the time of the Glorious Revolution, 1688 was the forerunner to the United States Bill of Rights.
4. True. Specifically, they agreed to covenant and combine themselves together into a civil "body politic." The principle of government by written agreement was accepted 16 years later by Roger Williams and his group who left Massachusetts to settle Providence, Rhode Island.

If you missed any of the above, reread Frame 2¹ before beginning Frame 3¹ on page 5.

Frame 3¹ continued

of Bourbon misrule in 1789, the same year that the U.S. Constitution took effect. At the historic Tennis Court Oath, recognized as the chronological starting point of the French Revolution, the rebellious citizens solemnly swore not to disband until they had a new and written constitution.

In the wake of the French Revolution and subsequent Napoleonic Wars, written constitutions were established (and often ruthlessly wiped out) all over Europe. Indeed, the history of Western Civilization from Waterloo (1815) to 1848 is the history of a group of strong, reactionary, absolutist powers, headed by the wily Count Metternich of Austria, combining to trample the flame of liberalism wherever it might crop up. In such a history it is difficult to overestimate the inspiration and influence of the successful and revolutionary governmental experiment in the United States.

Despite its disputed birth, the American Constitution has proven to be a healthy document, amazingly receptive to change, remarkably versatile, and extremely sensitive to the needs of the people it serves. As constitutions go, it has been extremely long lived. In its lifetime, for instance, the French have fashioned five Republics and two Empires. Designed for an agricultural colonial world of 3.8 million people, it has bridged the worlds of the Industrial Revolution

and the era of the B-747s without a serious generation or jet lag. It has survived Civil War, the Great Depression, the atomic bomb, and a population boom.

With its purview constantly under attack the Constitution has ever had the capacity and flexibility to "roll with the punch," or, to mash metaphors, "keep its finger on the public pulse." When Aaron Burr, vice president elect, almost stole the presidency in 1800 because of a muddy electoral clause, the 12th Amendment clarified the meaning. The Constitution has shot down "lame ducks" (20th Amendment), shut off the nation's liquor supply (18th), turned it on again (21st), and, as of this writing, the nation is considering saying "Yes, Ms." to the proposed 27th Equal Rights Amendment.

Yet the U.S. Constitution is far from a perfect instrument of government. Like the actions of a misbehaving son or daughter, its faults have often been embarrassing. Within the lifetime of most college graduates who read these lines, two costly wars (Korean and Vietnamese) have been fought without the built-in Congressional approval the Founding Fathers thought they had established.

New and knotty constitutional problems crop up constantly. In the second term of Richard Nixon, for instance, issues of executive privilege, the right of the president to impound funds appropriated by the Congress, the question of what constitutes an impeachable offense, and the propriety of law school admission policies which discriminate in favor of women and blacks have been fiercely debated. Tomorrow, the high court may be asked to consider whether the Congress can levy taxes on our colonists on the moon, whether a Yankee shortstop can "jump" to the Dodgers, or whether election judges may properly deny the vote to citizens who streak to the polls.

Is each of the following statements true or false?

_____ 1. The Fundamental Orders of Connecticut copied many of the provisions of the English Instrument of Government.

_____ 2. The Instrument of Government, the Mayflower Compact, the Compact executed by Roger Williams, and the Fundamental Orders of Connecticut were all legal documents.

_____ 3. European countries copied the United States action of establishing a written constitution.

_____ 4. The United States Constitution has proved to be extremely long lived and adaptable to change.

Now turn to Answer frame 3[1] on page 8 and check your responses.

Answer frame 3[1]

1. False. The document, the Fundamental Orders of Connecticut, was the first modern written constitution, and predated the English Instrument of Government by 14 years.
2. False. They were all illegal in one way or another, and may have been merely special conscious efforts to justify illegal actions.
3. True. Written constitutions were established all over Europe, but were often ruthlessly done away with.
4. True. It has been able to "roll with the punches," and (through the amending procedure) to keep up with the times.

If you missed any of the above, reread Frame 3[1] before beginning Chapter 2.

chapter 2

THE CONVENTION

Frame 1[2]

The men who came

"Dear God, do not send little men," a speaker is said to have warned the Connecticut legislature. From the 20/20 vision of hindsight, it is obvious that similar word must have filtered through to every state house.

It is equally clear that a lesser group of delegates could never have pulled off the world's greatest constitutional coup. The roll call at Philadelphia read like a "Who's Who of Post-revolutionary America"—a glittering display of American legal and political talent. In the spirited campaign for ratification, thousands of voters, unsure of this "radical" new document, were probably swayed by the integrity and patriotism of the men who drew up the Constitution.

Virginia, indeed, sent no little men, only giants. Among them George Washington, James Madison, George Mason, Judge Blair, George (Chancellor) Wythe, Edmund Randolph, and Patrick Henry.

Pennsylvania, too, chose with a vision which would sit well with the ages, contributing its irrepressible super patriot and elder statesman, Benjamin Franklin, who disregarded an aggravated case of gout to be carried in on a sedan chair; James Wilson, perhaps the keenest constitutional theorist west of Paris; and the polished Morris brothers, Robert and Gouverneur.

Connecticut's three man delegation was a triumph. "A Solomon, a Daniel, and a Saul," as one state chauvinist put it: Oliver Ellsworth, chief justice of the Connecticut Supreme Court; William Samuel Johnson, former justice of the state supreme court and holder of a Doctorate of Laws from Oxford; and Roger Sherman, nominal sponsor of the Connecticut Compromise which may have saved the Constitution.

No greater patriot nor abler civil servant answered the call than Alexander Hamilton of New York's three man delegation. Yet frustration sat with this West Indian born delegate to such an extent that he often stayed in bed. His fellow delegates were John Lansing and Robert Yates, a pair of political etceteras alongside the great Federalist. Jealous guardians of the principle of state sovereignty, Yates and Lansing outvoted Hamilton two to one on every vital issue. When Lansing and Yates packed their bags on July 5, never to return, Hamilton was still unable to cast a vote for New York. There was no longer a quorum in New York's delegation.

Maryland accredited a delegation headed by its attorney general, Luther Martin, who was to gain fame for his defense of Justice Chase in the celebrated trial of Aaron Burr.

Rufus King, most eloquent orator on the floor, and Elbridge Gerry of Massachusetts, William Paterson of New Jersey, John Rutledge and the two Pinckneys, C. C. and Charles, of South Carolina, and John Dickenson of Delaware are but a few of the better known men who gave up home and family to spend the summer of 1787 in blistering Philadelphia.

Of the 39 signers, two, Washington and Madison, would go on to serve double terms as president; six, Rutledge, Wilson, Blair, Dickenson, Paterson, and Ellsworth would become Supreme Court justices, with Ellsworth moving on to the chief justiceship. Two, Hamilton and James McHenry of Maryland, would become cabinet members. Others would serve as senators, congressmen, governors, and judges. Of the three who participated all the way but did not sign, Elbridge Gerry became vice president and Edmund Randolph twice served in cabinets.

Several thousand miles of ocean kept three distinguished statesmen away. Thomas Paine, whose *Common Sense* and *The Crisis* made him known as "the voice of the American Revolution," was in England, Thomas Jefferson was serving as minister to France, and John Adams was similarly occupied in London. Patrick Henry, elected a delegate, refused to serve, and Samuel Adams and John Hancock were not named as delegates.

The proceedings

The Convention was scheduled to open May 14, but only the home state delegates and those of Virginia were on hand. Financial difficulties, heavy rains, poor road conditions, and other reasons delayed the official opening until May 25 when nine state delegations, two more than required for a quorum, answered the roll.

But the delay was not a total loss. The Virginia and Pennsylvania delegations met informally almost daily and it was in this period that the famous Virginia Resolutions (later variously known as the Randolph Plan, the Virginia Plan, or the Large States Plan) were formulated.

The proceedings which were to establish the world's noblest democracy were hardly democratic. Troopers guarded the state house doors. A strict secrecy oath was imposed. No press credentials were honored. Delegates were overwhelmingly men of property and of the professions. There were no blacks, no Jews, no Indians, no women, no representatives of the working class.

Official records were not disclosed for 60 years. Even so, the cogent notes of James Madison, published 50 years later, have been of much greater historical value than the bloodless official *Journal* of minutes, motions, amendments, and procedural pronouncements.

Parliamentary politeness prevailed. The gentlemen addressed each other and the chair with old world courtesy and formality. In an entire summer of impassioned debate, there were no oaths, obscenities, vindictive personal attacks, or threats of filibuster. By agreement, once a delegate had addressed the Convention he could not again speak on that subject until all the delegates had been given a chance to speak. The rules banned whispering, or even reading a newspaper while a fellow delegate was speaking. The clerk did not take the "ayes" and "nays" of individual members, thus allowing for simple changes of mind, without embarrassment, at a later time. Votes were cast by *state*, and when even-numbered state delegations split, the state's vote was not counted.

So that they might speak freely and informally, the delegates often turned the Convention into a session of the committee of the whole. This was a centuries-old ploy of English Parliaments whereby the speaker would step down from the chair, removing the gavel or mace, symbolic of the monarchical presence and authority, and turn the meeting over to a surrogate (substitute) member. With the gavel removed, no official record would be taken and the king would not be informed. When George Washington stepped down in Philadelphia, Na-

thaniel Gorham of Massachusetts presided over the committee of the whole.

Of 74 delegates named by 12 state legislatures, only 55 presented credentials. Of these, 39 signed the final document on September 17. More than 60 percent were lawyers; 29 of the 39 signers were university graduates.

There were 79 working days of seven hours each, plus a great deal of "homework" at night. The Confederation Congress made no provision for payment. Some states provided remuneration; others did not. Fortunately, most delegates were wealthy. When New Hampshire could not afford to send representatives, John Langton agreed to pick up the tab.

Indicate whether each of the following statements is true or false by writing "T" or "F" in the space provided.

_____ 1. Truly great men attended the Constitutional Convention almost without exception.

_____ 2. All the delegates stayed the entire summer of 1787 and signed the Constitution.

_____ 3. The proceedings began when scheduled and were very democratic.

_____ 4. The behavior of some of the delegates on the floor of the convention was crude and impolite.

Now turn to Answer frame 1² on page 12 and check your responses.

Frame 2²

In Rhode Island, which was fearful of having to pay its considerable debts with a sound *national* currency, the agrarian majority was printing paper money by the ream in Providence and refused to send a delegation. "Rogue Island," as one of its many detractors called it, was also the last state to ratify, holding off until May 1790, 32 months after the Convention adjourned and 16 months after the Constitution became the law of the land. Even then, in the face of a congressional threat to sever commercial relations with the state, ratification squeaked through by a margin of only two votes.

At no time were more than 11 states represented in a single meeting, and seldom were there more than 30 delegates present. The fruitful work was performed in committee by about 12 men who were directed, cajoled, pushed, and inspired always by the intense and gifted dele-

gate from Virginia and true "father of the Constitution," James Madison.

To illustrate how a few men dominated, four men addressed the Convention a total of 640 times—Gouverneur Morris, 173; Wilson, 168; Madison, 161; and Sherman, 138. George Washington spoke only once.

Though the east chamber of the Pennsylvania state house was pleasant and reasonably cool, the weather was often intensely hot and humid, with scarcely enough breeze to riffle the cigar smoke. Not the least of the decisions was whether to open the windows, for the portholes which admitted the fresh air also let in the swarms of flies and mosquitoes which also seemed to be in summer-long convention in the City of Brotherly Love.

The 55 delegates came and went, absented by anger, poverty, frustration, disappointment, and hangover, or kept away by illness, personal affairs, and business interests. The New Hampshire delegation arrived July 23, delayed two months by the hole in the treasury. John Mercer of Maryland was the last delegate to present credentials, appearing on August 6 when much of the work was already accomplished.

Since voting was to be by states, there was no rule as to the number of delegates each state could send. Pennsylvania, perhaps because the expense was minimal for a delegate living at home, sent the most—eight. Virginia also named eight, but Patrick Henry, remarking that he "smelled a rat," remained at home and was not replaced.

Despite Ben Franklin's 81 years, it was a remarkably young group which gathered to represent a young nation of young people—a pattern totally out of step with the popular concept of a group of doddering, white-haired Founding Fathers. The country itself, if its birthday can be determined as July 4, 1776, was only 11 years old; more than half of its 4 million citizens were under 16 years of age, and the average age of the delegates was about 43. Of the 39 signers, 15 were in their 20s or early 30s.

Indicate whether each of the following statements is true or false.

_____ 1. Not all states even sent a delegation to the Convention.

_____ 2. The most fruitful work was not done on the floor of the Convention.

_____ 3. George Washington dominated the floor of the Convention by speaking about 200 times.

_____ 4. Each delegate had one vote, and each state had the same number of delegates.

Now turn to Answer frame 2² on page 12 and check your responses.

Frame 3²

Getting to work

The first couple of days were devoted to procedural matters. George Washington was elected presiding officer, William Jackson was named secretary, and a committee of rules was formed.

On May 29, in a three hour address that must go down as one of the most important in American history, Edmund Randolph, handsome 33-year-old governor of Virginia, formally presented the Virginia Plan calling for a strong central government which would exercise power over *individual citizens*. The Convention then resolved that the following day it would turn itself into a committee of the whole to debate the Virginia (or Randolph) Plan.

This was an historic decision. It meant that the Articles of Confederation instructions were out the window. It meant that the sham of pretending to amend the Articles was over—squelched in one brisk, unanimous motion. It meant that the Federalists had carried the day. It would come to mean the end of loose Confederation rule.

From May 30 to June 19 the committee of the whole debated the merits of the Virginia Plan, threshing out each point line by line, many times word by word. The Virginia Plan called for:

1. A legislature of *two houses,* members of whom would be elected on the basis of the number of free inhabitants or of wealth. The lower house would be elected by the people; the upper house would be elected by the lower house; members would not be eligible for reelection.

2. A chief executive, who might be either an individual or a committee, elected by members of the two Houses; the executive would not be eligible for reelection.

3. A supreme court of limited jurisdiction. The executive and supreme court would share jointly a "revision" or veto power.

4. The amending power to be vested in the *people,* not in the two houses or in the executive.

5. The legislature would have power to annul state laws.

Answer frame 1²

1. True. The roll call read like a "Who's Who of Postrevolutionary America"—a glittering display of American legal and political talent whose integrity and patriotism could not be questioned.
2. False. About 30 delegates did not attend or left before the work was finished (for example, Yates and Lansing from New York). Even of those who participated to the end, three did not sign the Constitution.
3. False. The proceedings were delayed one week (during which time the Virginia Plan was formulated), and the proceedings were very *undemocratic*. Delegates were wealthy and largely from the professions.
4. False. The delegates addressed each other and the chair with old world courtesy and formality. There were no oaths, obscenities, or vindictive personal attacks.

If you missed any of the above, reread Frame 1² before beginning Frame 2² on page 10.

Answer frame 2²

1. True. Rhode Island refused to send a delegation and was the last state to ratify (16 months after the Constitution became the law of the land). Ratification only passed by two votes even after a congressional threat to sever commercial relations with the state.
2. True. It was performed in committee by about 12 men under the leadership of James Madison (who came to be known as the "father of the Constitution").
3. False. Washington spoke only *once*, but presided over the Convention. Morris, Wilson, Madison, and Sherman dominated the floor of the Convention.
4. False. Each *state* had one vote, and there was no rule as to the number of delegates each state could send (Pennsylvania sent the most—8).

If you missed any of the above, reread Frame 2² before beginning Frame 3² on page 11.

Frame 3² continued

On June 11 the Convention approved proportional representation for both houses. This was the shocker that galvanized the small states into action. On June 15 William Paterson of New Jersey requested permission to present the New Jersey Plan which:

1. Gave a congress, in addition to its present rights, the power to tax, to regulate interstate commerce, and to bring reluctant states into line by coercion.
2. Provided for *all states to be represented equally* in the legislature.
3. Created an executive subject to control by the several states.

In practice, the New Jersey Plan would merely have embroidered upon the Articles of Confederation. It was defeated, seven to three, after spirited debate. Nevertheless, the small state delegates were far from surrender. United,

they held the votes which would force an acceptable compromise.

For the record, two other plans were presented. On May 29 Charles Pinckney presented his personal plan for union. It was never seriously considered. A generation later, however, Pinckney would claim that his proposal bore a remarkable resemblance to the Constitution that was finally drafted. History has looked upon this claim as a fraud.

Alexander Hamilton also presented a plan. An admirer of the British system, Hamilton would have created, among other things, an upper house and an executive elected for life, patterned after the British House of Lords and Monarch. The Hamilton Plan failed to attract a single supporter.

Tension heightened when, after defeat of the Paterson proposal, representation for both houses on a population basis was again broached. For two days Maryland's alarmed Luther Martin expounded on the necessity for state equality in any confederated network.

The crisis was at hand. It was give or go home. Franklin suggested appeal to a higher authority, moving that a chaplain be hired to begin each session with a prayer. But everybody knew there were no funds for this purpose.

Finally, a suggestion was adopted that a committee composed of one member from each state be appointed to work out a compromise. Rugged states' righters such as Martin, Yates, and Paterson were among those named by their states to slug it out in committee.

Out of the committee report of July 5, the Great Compromise was hatched. Though often called the Connecticut Compromise, because of the work of Ellsworth and Sherman, the term is a misnomer. Many others contributed as much or more. It provided:

For equal representation in the upper house.

For proportional membership in the lower house on the basis of one member per 40,000 inhabitants. Population, not property, was to be the sole basis of representation.

Acceptance of the Connecticut Compromise was the turning point of the convention. Many problems remained, but reasonable men now could find reasonable ways of surmounting them. Throughout the give and take of those sultry summer days, a single theme hummed through the minds of the small-state and states' rights delegates: "We have not sold our people down the stream; no matter what happens we will have two votes in the upper house."

When all points were resolved, the 23 Articles were given to a committee of style, composed of William Samuel Johnson, chairman, Rufus King, Alexander Hamilton, James Madison, and Gouverneur Morris. The committee labored from September 8 to 12, reducing the 23 Articles to seven, simplifying, clarifying, changing the order, but retaining the original intent.

All members of the committee had a hand in the preparation of the details of the completed draft, but it was the 35-year-old Gouverneur Morris who is credited with providing the clear, graceful, legalistic prose which still distinguishes this remarkable document. Tall, aristocratic, member of a wealthy and socially prominent New York family, openly contemptuous of democracy, Morris labored over the phraseology with the mind of a skilled lawyer, the heart of a philosopher, and the soul of a poet.

The completed draft was presented to the Convention on September 12, and immediately drew scores of objections—Elbridge Gerry alone found 11. After much debate but little alteration the Constitution of the United States was accepted and signed on September 17 by 39 of the 42 members present. Only Gerry, Mason, and Randolph declined to affix signatures. With a covering letter by George Washington, it was sent to the Articles of Confederation Congress, where it was received with considerable shock.

But the real job was just beginning.

Is each of the following statements true or false?

_____ 1. Consideration of the Virginia Plan meant that the instructions given to the delegates to merely revise the Articles of Confederation were not going to be followed.

_____ 2. At first the delegates approved proportional representation for *both* houses.

_____ 3. The New Jersey Plan was the small state plan calling for all states to be represented equally in the legislature and eventually led to the Great Compromise position of having equal state representation in the upper house.

_____ 4. The Constitution, with a covering letter by George Washington, was sent to the Articles of Confederation Congress where it was received with enthusiastic support.

Now turn to Answer frame 3² on page 14 to check your responses.

Answer frame 3²

1. True. This is the real significance of the Virginia Plan, since it was never adopted by the delegates.
2. True. But later, in the Great Compromise, this was changed to equal representation in the upper house (the Senate) and proportional representation in the lower house (the House of Representatives). The Great Compromise was the turning point of the Convention.
3. True. The Jersey Plan was as described. The small state delegates were united on the issue of equal state representation and held the votes to force an acceptable compromise.
4. False. It was received with considerable shock. The delegates had not performed the assigned task of merely recommending revisions of the Articles of Confederation, but had instead conceived a totally new and "radical" document.

If you missed any of the above, reread Frame 3² before beginning Chapter 3.

chapter 3

RATIFICATION

Frame 1³

The Confederation Congress looked upon the new Constitution with all the enthusiasm a firmly entrenched board of directors might look upon a surprise proposal to reorganize the corporation. Nevertheless, but without a kind word or a "God bless you," the Congress, reinforced by the return of ten of its members who had been delegates at Philadelphia, promptly voted to submit the proposal to the several states.

The state legislatures, in turn, could vote to call ratification conventions composed of delegates chosen by the people. Delegates were not always bound by the votes of their constituents and occasionally changed their minds after listening to the debates or the persuasion of fellow delegates.

Those who favored the Constitution became known as Federalists. Those opposed were called Antifederalists, a negative term which many resented.

There is no question but that ratification by "We, the people" was a noble concept, establishing the fountainhead of sovereignty out of deep faith in the will of the great democratic majority. But many contend that it was less of a noble concept than a practical political necessity.

"Suppose the Constitution was submitted to the Confederation Congress or to the state legislatures," theorized one skeptic. "Do you think those gentlemen would have voted themselves out of a job?"

Article Five, the amending article, required

ratification by nine states. With Rhode Island's position predetermined (true to form, she did not call a convention until long after the question was settled), this meant 9 out of 12, not 9 out of 13.

Who could vote

The vote for ratification of the noblest of all democratic constitutions was every bit as undemocratic as the proceedings of the convention which drafted that Constitution.

It must be remembered that these were state referendums. The emancipated suffrage proposed in the new Constitution had no bearing in these elections. State regulations applied. In 11 states, property qualifications would disfranchise from one fourth to two thirds of all adult males. Residency and religious restrictions would further cut into these figures. In Virginia, South Carolina, and Georgia, blacks were excluded. The religious requirements, known as Test Acts, often disfranchised Roman Catholics; in Georgia, atheists were denied the suffrage.

Since women were never considered as potential voters, the various restrictions sometimes excluded five sixths of all adults. Still, apathy and ignorance, particularly in the hinterlands, were the most effective censors, keeping from 60 to 80 percent of the privileged eligible minority from the polls. Of Pennsylvania's 430,000 citizens, 70,000 were eligible and only 13,000 voted; of Maryland's 320,000 residents, 25,000 were privileged to cast ballots, but only 6,000 bothered to do so. More than half of these were from the populated districts, primarily Baltimore, where the maritime interests looked forward to pleasant sailing under a single flag which would promote free-flowing trade.

All this in the most important election in the history of the United States!

Only one state, New York, granted general manhood suffrage for the Constitutional referendum. And this for a good reason. The patrician class of New York overwhelmingly opposed the Constitution. They believed they could control the ballots of enough servants, sharecroppers, tenants, and employees to swing defeat. Indeed, if ballots had been counted individually, the Constitution could never have made it

in New York. But the Poughkeepsie Convention was something less than a textbook example of representative democracy at work. The area we now roughly call metropolitan New York, with fewer than 90,000 citizens, was represented by 23 delegates; the "upstate" area, representing more than a quarter million people, had only 40.

The special interests

The campaign for approval by the states raged over a ten month period, roughly from October 1787, when the first legislatures met to set dates and issue calls for conventions, to the following August, by which time 11 states had ratified. "Raged" seems the proper verb, for emotions ran high and the participants played for keeps. A new way of life hung in the balance. Cherished prerogatives would have to be surrendered. Many believed that the dearly purchased freedoms of the War of Revolution would be endangered.

Quickly, the Founding Fathers perceived that it was one thing to put a new Constitution down on a piece of paper and something else to sell that document to a nation of skeptical buyers. All the forces and special interests which interacted at the Philadelphia Convention made themselves known in the campaign, plus many more: creditors who wanted payment in hard money and debtors who wished to pay off in devalued paper; manufacturers, planters, merchants, slaveholders, and seagoing interests; men who feared the Indians; men who wished to grab cheap western land; men who did not want the West colonized; people who exacted a living collecting river tolls and people who wanted to sail goods toll free; lawyers who stood to lose lucrative state contracts; congressmen who could be ratified right out of a job; rural people who feared the intolerance of metropolis ballots; citizens who feared their liberties would be endangered under a law of the land which contained no mention of a bill of rights; citizens who feared that members of Congress would be too far removed from their constituents; and citizens who feared that the ten square mile district to be set aside as the permanent home of the federal government would become a walled fortress from which squadrons of federal soldiers would march out to enforce federal regulations and the payment of federal taxes.

James Wilson summarized the opposition in this manner: "Every person who either enjoys or expects to enjoy a piece of profit under the present establishment will object to the proposed innovation."

Generally, the coastal areas would vote "aye" and the interior "nay"; small states, unable to exist independently and pleased with the compromise which gave them equal representation in the Senate, would approve more readily and with greater majorities than their big-state brothers; city dwellers, merchants, plantation owners, real estate speculators, people of affluence, and people who dealt in interstate commerce were inclined to favor. So were those who feared the British in Canada, the French in Louisiana, and the Spanish in Florida.

Laborers, small farmers, villagers, and the people of the frontier were usually opposed. Farmers, believing their fortunes (and mortgages) were tied to the adulterated dollar, opposed the sound money features which constitutionalism was certain to bring. Many "squatters" feared they might have to pay for lands which they had merely preempted. And they looked upon the professional land grabbers, who might be encouraged by the Constitution, as they might look upon skunks in their hen houses.

There were enough exceptions to these patterns, however, to make such generalizations dangerous. New York, North Carolina, and Rhode Island were coastal states with strong Antifederalist sentiments. Some interior communities dependent upon the free flow of river traffic were militantly Federalist. Backwoods Georgia, for reasons we shall see, favored ratification just as eagerly as the tidewater (coastal) region.

The cards of ratification were stacked in favor of the Federalists. America was a rural nation. Bad roads and the sheer nuisance of hitching up Old Dobbin would keep thousands of Antifederalist farmers away from the polls, while poor communications and necessity of working long hours in the fields discouraged any organized Antifederalist campaigning in agricultural communities.

Even the weatherman dealt from the bottom of the deck. Wherever bad weather prevailed on election day, the rural vote was affected to a greater extent than that of the city.

The formula for selecting delegates also served the Federalist cause. Delegates to the state constitutional conventions were selected on the same proportional basis as were members of state assemblies. With few exceptions, rural and backwater areas were grossly underrepresented in the state assemblies, and this representation would carry over in the state ratification conventions.

Indicate whether each of the following statements is true or false by writing "T" or "F" in the space provided.

_____ 1. All 13 states had to ratify the Constitution before it could become the law of the land.

_____ 2. Voting in the state referendums was very undemocratic.

_____ 3. Other than in Rhode Island there was very little opposition to the new Constitution.

_____ 4. The conditions of voting favored the Federalists, who favored ratification.

Now turn to Answer frame 1³ on page 18 and check your responses.

Frame 2[3]

The Federalist Papers

From the hundreds of speeches, sermons, debates, pamphlets, editorials, books and letters to the editor, one enduring piece of literature emerged. A series of 85 essays aimed at persuading New York voters to favor the Constitution began appearing in the New York press on October 27, 1787, and continued periodically until May. They were widely reprinted. Under the *nom de plume* of "Publius," the essays were the work of John Jay, who wrote 5, Madison, who probably wrote 29, and Hamilton, usually credited with authorship of 51.

As clear, reasoned statements of the anatomy and metabolism of representative government, *The Federalist Papers* have no peer in world literature. Judges, congressmen, presidents, and diplomats have used them as guidelines for almost 200 years. American political scientists refer to them as they would the Bible. They have been translated into many languages, studied worldwide, and have been influential in the formation of many modern constitutional forms of government.

Yet it is one of the ironies of history that *The Federalist Papers* probably had little influence in their time. In 1787, as in 1975, few voters were swayed by thoughtful, intellectual, low-key reasoning. Slogans, epithets, warnings, ballyhoo, half-truths, and appeal to prejudice probably persuaded more voters than these truly classic political analyses.

Richard Henry Lee's *Letters of a Federalist Farmer* was probably the finest analysis of the Antifederalist position.

Off to a good start

Three states ratified unanimously: Delaware (first to ratify) on December 7, New Jersey (third) on December 18th, and Georgia (fourth) on January 2.

Georgia. One clause in the preamble: (to) "provide for the common defense" was the bait that hooked Georgia. Savannah was a fortified city and the countryside shivered in fear of the Creek Indians. Others might debate theory and sovereignty and liberties infringed upon. Geor-gians needed the new Constitution and friendly federal troops—on the double.

George Washington clearly foresaw the issue: "If a weak State with the Indians on its back and the Spanish on its flank does not see the necessity of a General Government there must I think be wickedness or insanity in the way."

Connecticut. Connecticut was fifth to approve (January 9) and no one summarized the advantages to the state better than Oliver Ellsworth. Pointing out Connecticut's geographical position, he noted that New York collected possibly £80,000 in import duties annually and that Connecticut paid approximately one third of this amount. He also recalled how Connecticut promptly paid her wartime requisition taxes under the Articles of Confederation while other states reneged and got away with it under an impotent central authority. The vote was 128 to 40.

The tough ones

The larger states had more to lose and more people to vent their feelings than the smaller states. Thus, the most bitter and most newsworthy campaigns for ratification took place in Virginia, Pennsylvania, Massachusetts, and New York.

Pennsylvania. Pennsylvania was first to hear of the Constitution, first to call a ratification convention, and was beaten by Delaware by only a few days for the honor of being first to ratify.

Thomas Mifflin, a delegate to the Constitutional Convention, gave the Pennsylvania legislature a sneak preview of the new document. On September 18, the day after the Constitutional Convention adjourned, he read the proposed document to the unicameral Pennsylvania legislature. Reactions were instantaneous and violent on both sides.

George Clymer, a member of the Pennsylvania legislature who had been a delegate, made the motion to call a state convention within 24 hours after the Confederation Congress sent the Constitution to the states. The votes for passage clearly existed. But with adjournment set for the following day, and with an election around the corner, Antifederalists in the assembly plotted

Answer frame 1³

1. False. Ratification by nine states was required. And since Rhode Island was very much opposed, this meant 9 out of 12 rather than 9 out of 13.
2. True. State regulations then in effect applied to voting procedures. Only a very small percentage (for example about 2 percent in Maryland) of the residents qualified to vote and chose to do so. Only New York State granted general manhood suffrage for the Constitutional referendum.
3. False. There was substantial opposition from all sorts of special interest groups. As James Wilson said, "Every person who either enjoys or expects to enjoy a piece of profit under the present establishment will object to the proposed innovation."
4. True. Bad roads, bad weather, and long working hours kept many rural people away from the polls. These people were generally Antifederalist. Also, the method of selecting delegates to the state constitutional conventions resulted in the underrepresentation of rural and backwater areas.

If you missed any of the above, reread Frame 1³ before beginning Frame 2³ on page 17.

Frame 2³ continued

the politics of procrastination. The November election, they hoped, might return an Assembly opposed to ratification.

A recess was achieved and when the afternoon session was called to order enough Antifederalists were absent to thwart a quorum call. The sergeant at arms, sent to fetch the absentees, reported he was unable to "haul them out of their hole."

On Saturday, the 29th, following a night of drinking and demonstrating, a band of overzealous citizens battered the windows of "Mr. Boyd's house," an Antifederalist hangout, and literally hauled two struggling assemblymen to the state house, where their sullen, silent presence was properly recorded by the clerk. With a quorum thus obtained, a convention call was issued by a vote of 45 to 2.

The campaign that followed was noisy and violent, as small townsmen, farmers, and backwoodsmen voiced their uncertainties. The doddering Franklin assured the doubters that their fears were groundless, but it was the eloquent and statesmanlike James Wilson who proved to be Pennsylvania's strongest and most effective champion of constitutionalism. He dwelt on the many checks and balances designed to thwart any grab for power by a single man or conspiratial group of small states. He noted that the Senate, where the small states might gang up on the large ones, would be unable to railroad

legislation without consent of the House, where Pennsylvania would wield the power of several small states. The president would have veto power over the Congress and the Congress in turn held a sort of reverse veto power over the president.

Despite the considerable stir created by opponents, the Constitution carried handily, 46 to 23, in the roll call of December 12, making Pennsylvania the second state to ratify.

Massachusetts. There could be no union without populous Massachusetts, where a bitter constitutional tea party was waged for four weeks.

The province of Maine, which hoped to break away from Massachusetts and become an independent state, was solidly opposed. So were the delegates from the Berkshire area, where Captain Daniel Shays and his men had so recently raised so much turbulence (29 of the delegates had fought with Shays); so were the paper money people, the small farmers, and most of the tiny inland towns.

The coastal towns were Federalist. And the Federalists, with such stalwarts as Rufus King, Nathaniel Gorham, and former governor Bowdoin, were better organized.

Of the 355 delegates, 60 percent or more probably came to Boston on January 9 opposed. If the Federalists were to have any chance at all, they would need the hearty support of

Samuel Adams, their already legendary Revolutionary hero, and of Governor John Hancock, of Declaration immortality. Adams was tepid; Hancock aloof and cool, preferring to wait and see which way the political tides might flow.

After three weeks of heated debate a delegation headed by Adams climbed Beacon Hill to knock on the door of the wealthy and gouty Hancock. They proposed that the governor declare for ratification on condition that a series of amendments be tacked on for the consideration of the Congress.

The price for Hancock's support? The presidency, if Virginia failed to ratify or if Washington declined to serve. Otherwise, the vice presidency or, some say, the promise of Bowdoin's support in the next governor's race.

Hancock agreed to the bribe and, his feet swathed in bandages, was carried theatrically to the rostrum to make his "Conciliatory Proposition" as though it were his own brainchild. Adams, still the darling of both sides, seconded the resolution to consider the amendments, and a few days later added several of his own.

The Constitution carried on February 6, 187 to 168, making Massachusetts the sixth state to ratify. Considering that certain small towns, normally Antifederalist, were denied delegates because they were in arrears to the state treasury, and that a swing of ten votes would have brought defeat, and that the law of the land could not have carried without Massachusetts approval, it can properly be said that the good ship *Constitution* almost floundered off Plymouth Rock before it ever got out of the harbor.

If John Hancock were indeed promised the vice presidency in return for his support, he was the victim of the first political double-cross in the history of the new nation.

And the "Massachusetts formula"—the idea of suggesting amendments along with ratification—became the vehicle which was to carry the Constitution past some difficult roadblocks.

Maryland. Maryland became the seventh state to ratify despite the harangues of Luther Martin and the doubts of Samuel Chase. Federalists dominated the convention, which first met at Annapolis on April 21. Following the example set by Massachusetts, a series of amendments, finally whittled down to 13, were suggested, but no formal action of approval or disapproval was taken. The vote to ratify was 63 to 11, on April 28.

South Carolina. South Carolina, planter country, became number eight on May 23, approving by a vote of 149 to 73 with the support of John Rutledge and the powerful Pickneys.

Indicate whether each of the following statements is true or false.

_____ 1. *The Federalist Papers* were outstanding in quality and were very influential in bringing about ratification.

_____ 2. Delaware, New Jersey, and Georgia were the first three states to ratify.

_____ 3. John Hancock may have been given a false promise to secure his support for ratification in Massachusetts.

_____ 4. The "Massachusetts formula" was important in bringing about final ratification.

Now turn to Answer frame 2³ on page 20 and check your responses.

Frame 3³

New Hampshire. New Hampshire was but one of several states which probably would not have ratified had there been one general election day on which no state knew how the sister states would vote. Shortly after the convention met on February 15, an unofficial sounding showed the Antifederalists commanded a majority of four votes over the Federalist forces from the coastal and Connecticut River areas.

After ten days of fruitless discussion, the dele-

Answer frame 2³

1. False. As excellent as these papers were, they probably had *little* influence in their time. They have had a profound influence on later generations however.
2. False. Delaware, Pennsylvania, and New Jersey were the first three states to ratify. Georgia was fourth and Connecticut was fifth.
3. True. There is speculation that he was offered the presidency (if Virginia failed to ratify or if Washington declined to serve) or the vice presidency. If he was offered the vice presidency he was probably double-crossed.
4. True. This mechanism was to propose a series of amendments along with ratification and was used in both Massachusetts and Maryland (and later in Virginia) to help achieve ratification.

If you missed any of the above, reread Frame 2³ before beginning Frame 3³ on page 19.

Frame 3³ continued

gates could only agree to disagree. Recessing until June 3 (a date later set back to June 17), they returned home to seek further instructions from their constituents. When the convention finally reconvened Maryland and South Carolina had ratified and the option strings around New Hampshire's neck had tightened.

And still the vote was close! On June 21, 1878, at 1 P.M., little New Hampshire by the margin of 57 to 47 sneaked into the federal bosom, having absolutely no place else to go. Before the first toast was drunk, the clerk carefully noted the hour of ratification so that history would know whether New Hampshire or Virginia would have the honor of being the ninth and "clincher" state.

Virginia. Virginia, of course, did not make up its mind until four days later and then came perilously close to scuttling the entire ship of state. Virginia, largest state by far, sent a star-spangled cast of delegates to the convention which opened on June 2.

Patrick Henry, evangelistic in his opposition, dominated the proceedings to such an extent that his speeches took up more than 100 of the 600 pages of the official record, and the press referred to the Antifederalists as "Henryites." Others opposed were George Mason, Colonel William Grayson, Richard Henry Lee, James Monroe, and John Tyler, whose son was later to serve as tenth president.

The Federalist lineup was equally impressive: Edmund Pendleton, elected presiding officer, Chancellor Wythe, James Madison, John Marshall, and Light Horse Harry Lee. They were joined by the influential Governor Edmund Randolph who, though he had declined to become a signer at Philadelphia, jolted the antifederalists and incurred the withering wrath of Patrick Henry when he declared that he could not obstruct progress by opposing ratification. The Federalists also worked with the comforting knowledge that the squire of Mount Vernon, George Washington, and the sage of Monticello, Thomas Jefferson, blessed their cause.

With this most distinguished cast, the largest and most important state staged the most impressive convention, the most statesmanlike debates, the clearest and most wide-ranging pronouncements of the rival philosophies of government. With both sides well organized and almost equal in strength, the sessions trumpeted on for more than three weeks while the fate of the nation hung in the balance. For if Virginia turned thumbs down, New York would certainly follow suit, and recalcitrant Rhode Island and North Carolina would have been only too happy to make it a foursome. Indeed, Governor Randolph received a letter from Governor Clinton of New York which virtually promised that if Virginia would reject, New York almost certainly would follow her example. But Randolph did not make the letter public until after the final vote had been taken. History can only conjecture what its effect might have been.

One of the most persistent Antifederalist arguments—one in which Thomas Jefferson sympathized philosophically from his minister's post in Paris—was the lack of a bill of rights. Again, the "Massachusetts formula" probably saved the day. It was agreed that a set of 29 proposed amendments would be attached to the official report. With this concession, the crucial vote was taken on June 25 and ratification approved, 89 to 79. Consider that a change of six votes might have detoured the course of American history! The possibility of a United States where George Washington and Thomas Jefferson were regarded as aliens was dissipated.

New York. New York was an Antifederalist nest. And why not? From her strategic position commanding a great harbor and crucial waterways, she was able to impose heavy interstate tolls that virtually canceled the need for real estate taxes. The new government would strike down this windfall. It was no accident that the Antifederalist majority at the Poughkeepsie Convention was a solid 46 to 19.

Governor George Clinton and the two runaway delegates from the Philadelphia Convention, Lansing and Yates, joined with Melancton Smith, Thomas Tredwell, and Samuel Jones to lead the opposition. Their strength was clearly reflected when Clinton was chosen presiding officer. The affluent squirearchy of the Hudson Valley opened up their purses to defeat the new federal menace.

What happened in New York was also certain to influence the decision in North Carolina and Rhode Island, where the Constitution was equally unpopular.

Had the convention met in December or January, the Constitution could not have carried. But by July, the new law of the land was already a reality. Then came the knockout blow —news that Virginia had ratified. Cleverly, Alexander Hamilton posed still another threat to New Yorkers who pondered whether they could live outside the Constitution.

"Of course you realize," he told the convention, "that if you refuse to ratify then New York City will secede from the state and ratify by itself, and where will the Empire State be without its crown jewel?"

With seven Antifederalists abstaining, New York stamped a hesitant "OK" on July 26 by a vote of 30 to 27. There was nothing else to do.

North Carolina. North Carolina, rural and reactionary, did not meet until the Fourth of July, by which time ten states were already in the federal barn and New York was trudging reluctantly toward the stable. Still, the farmer and frontier elements were skeptical. Technically, North Carolina did not reject outright, but *refused to ratify* until a lengthy list of proposed amendments could be assured. This action was taken on July 21, 184 to 83, whereupon the convention recessed. On November 21 North Carolina reconvened, reconsidered, 194 to 77, and sneaked in the back door.

Rhode Island. If North Carolina was "reluctant," Rhode Island was downright obstinate. The only state to refuse to call a ratifying convention stayed out in the pasture throughout the year 1789 and well into the following year. In the spring elections of 1890, the paper money adherents in the legislature suffered a setback. In the face of federal threats, the new state assembly quickly squeaked through a call for a convention, which approved the Constitution on May 29, 1791.

Rhode Island still did not enter graciously. The vote was 34 to 32. A single "Rogue Islander" could have forced a tie and kept the state out of the Union. But that single vote was not forthcoming. The 13 original colonies were now 13 states.

TABLE 1
Ratification of the Constitution

State	Order of ratification	Date of ratification	Vote
Delaware	1	December 7, 1787	30–0*
Pennsylvania	2	December 12, 1787	46–23
New Jersey	3	December 18, 1787	38–0*
Georgia	4	January 2, 1788	26–0*
Connecticut	5	January 9, 1788	128–40
Massachusetts	6	February 6, 1788	187–168
Maryland	7	April 28, 1788	63–11
South Carolina	8	May 23, 1788	149–73
New Hampshire	9	June 21, 1788	57–47
Virginia	10	June 25, 1788	89–79
New York	11	July 26, 1788	30–27
North Carolina	12	November 21, 1788	194–77
Rhode Island	13	May 29, 1790	34–32

Source: Data taken from Richard B. Morris, ed. *Encyclopedia of American History.* Rev. ed. (New York: Harper & Brothers, 1961), and Clinton Rossiter, *1787 The Grand Convention* (New York: The Macmillan Company, 1966).
* These votes were unanimous.

Is each of the following statements true or false?

_____ 1. New Hampshire probably would not have ratified had it been unaware that eight other states had already ratified.

_____ 2. Patrick Henry, George Mason, James Monroe, and John Tyler achieved ratification in the state of Virginia.

_____ 3. If Virginia had not ratified, the Constitution would not have become the law of the land.

_____ 4. In New York State opposition to ratification was very strong.

Now turn to Answer frame 3³ on page 24 and check your responses.

chapter 4

THE CONSTITUTION OF THE UNITED STATES*

Frame 1⁴

THE CONSTITUTION

Preamble—We, the people of the United States, in order to form a more perfect Union, establish justice, insure domestic tranquility, provide for the common defence, promote the general welfare, and secure the blessings of liberty to ourselves and our posterity, do ordain and establish this Constitution for the United States of America.

---

* Subject headings, which do not appear in the original document, are modifications of those to be found in *State of New Hampshire Manual for the General Court* (Concord, N.H., 1969), pp. 15–42.

Explanations and Comments

Preamble—The most famous, and probably the most perfect, sentence in American documentary history. The first 7 words establish the source of all sovereignty. The next 45 distill the essence of millions of words of philosophical debate. The Preamble is a statement of purpose, a reason for being, a rationale for presenting the script by which Americans would forever consent to be governed.

Primarily the work of Gouvernor Morris, the Preamble is a literary as well as political triumph. The verbs are crisp, dynamic, and purposeful, the goals summarize the dreams of freedom lovers everywhere, and the poetic cadence is most noticeable when the lines are set in verse form and read aloud.

The first three Articles deal, in turn, with the three branches of government; and the numerical se-

THE CONSTITUTION (cont.)

Explanations and Comments

quence (Article One—Legislative; Article Two—Executive; Article Three—Judicial) distinctly reflects the importance of these branches in the minds of the Founding Fathers. The Legislative was looked upon as the preeminent branch—closest to the people, most responsive to their wishes. The 20th century practice by which the Executive proposes extensive Legislative programs and the Judicial arm holds life and death power in its interpretation of every debatable phrase was probably never dreamed of by the men who drew up the Constitution.

ARTICLE ONE

ARTICLE ONE—The Legislative

SECTION 1

Legislative powers vested in Congress—All legislative powers herein granted shall be vested in a Congress of the United States, which shall consist of a Senate and House of Representatives.

SECTION 2

Composition of the House of Representatives—1. The House of Representatives shall be composed of members chosen every second year by the people of the several States, and the electors in each State shall have the qualifications requisite for electors of the most numerous branch of the State Legislature.

Thus the *state* sets qualifications for electors (voters) in a federal election. Certain acts of Congress and certain amendments (14th, 17th, 19th, 26th) have since abridged state authority.

Qualifications of Representatives—2. No Person shall be a Representative who shall not have attained to the age of twenty-five years, and been seven years a citizen of the United States, and who shall not, when elected, be an inhabitant of that State in which he shall be chosen.

Note that the Constitution uses the term "inhabitant" instead of "legal resident," and that senators also must merely be "inhabitants." (Sec. 3, paragraph 3). Such a distinction enabled Robert Kennedy to be elected senator from New York in 1964. An "inhabitant" of New York but still a "registered voter" and probably a legal resident of Massachusetts, Kennedy had not lived in New York long enough to meet the state's voting requirements. College students, and members of the armed forces are often confronted with the problem of "legal residency" status.

Apportionment of Representatives and census—3. [Representatives and direct taxes shall be apportioned among the several States which may be included within this Union, according to their respective numbers, which shall be determined by adding to the whole number of free persons, including those bound to service for a term of years and excluding Indians not taxed, three fifths of all other persons.] The actual enumeration shall be made within three years

The clause enclosed by brackets has been obsolete since passage of the 14th Amendment, ratified in 1868.

"Other persons"—a fancy term for slaves.

Answer frame 3³

1. True. When the New Hampshire state convention first met, the Antifederalists had a majority of four votes over the Federalists. Only after eight other states had ratified did New Hampshire decide to follow.
2. False. They all actively opposed ratification. But those favoring ratification included Edmund Pendleton, Chancellor Wythe, James Madison, John Marshall, Light Horse Harry Lee, and Governor Edmund Randolph (with backing by George Washington and Thomas Jefferson).
3. False. Nine states had already ratified thus making the Constitution the law of the land. But New York, Rhode Island, and North Carolina probably would not have ratified. The young nation of nine states may not have survived this development.
4. True. The Constitution would have been rejected had it not been for Virginia ratifying and the fact that Alexander Hamilton pointed out that New York City would secede from the state and ratify by itself if the state refused to ratify.

If you missed any of the above, reread Frame 3³ before beginning Chapter 4 on page 22.

Frame 1⁴ continued
THE CONSTITUTION (cont.)

Explanations and Comments

after the first meeting of the Congress of the United States, and within every subsequent term of ten years, in such manner as they shall by law direct. The number of Representatives shall not exceed one for every thirty thousand, but each State shall have at least one Representative; and until such enumeration shall be made, the State of New Hampshire shall be entitled to choose three, Massachusetts eight, Rhode-Island and Providence Plantations one, Connecticut five, New York six, New Jersey four, Pennsylvania eight, Delaware one, Maryland six, Virginia ten, North Carolina five, South Carolina five, and Georgia three.

Vacancies—4. When vacancies happen in the representation from any State, the Executive Authority thereof shall issue writs of election to fill such vacancies.

The Governor.

Selection of officers; impeachment—5. The House of Representatives shall choose their Speaker and other officers; and shall have the sole power of impeachment.

Indicate whether each of the following statements is true or false by writing "T" or "F" in the space provided.

_____ 1. The Preamble sets out the purposes for establishing the Constitution of the United States of America.

_____ 2. Legislative powers are vested in the president of the United States.

_____ 3. A candidate for a House seat must be an inhabitant of that state in which he seeks election, must have been a United States citizen for at least seven years, must be at least 25 years of age, and shall serve a two year term if elected.

_____ 4.   The House of Representatives selects its Speaker and other officers, but the Senate has the sole power of impeaching these leaders.

Now turn to Answer frame 1[4] on page 26 and check your responses.

Frame 2[4]

THE CONSTITUTION (cont.)
SECTION 3

The Senate—[1. The Senate of the United States shall be composed of two Senators from each State, chosen by the Legislature thereof, for six years; and each Senator shall have one vote.]

Classification of Senators; vacancies—2. Immediately after they shall be assembled in consequence of the first election, they shall be divided as equally as may be into three classes. The seats of the Senators of the first class shall be vacated at the expiration of the second year, of the second class at the expiration of the fourth year, and of the third class at the expiration of the sixth year, so that one third may be chosen every second year; and if vacancies happen by resignation, or otherwise, during the recess of the Legislature of any State, the Executive thereof may make temporary appointments [until the next meeting of the Legislature, which shall then fill such vacancies.]

Qualification of Senators—3. No person shall be a Senator who shall not have attained to the age of thirty years, and been nine years a citizen of the United States, and who shall not, when elected, be an inhabitant of that State for which he shall be chosen.

Vice President—4. The Vice President of the United States shall be President of the Senate, but shall have no vote, unless they be equally divided.

Senate Officers; President pro tempore—5. The Senate, shall choose their other officers, and also a President pro tempore, in the absence of the Vice President, or when he shall exercise the office of President of the United States.

Senate to try impeachment—6. The Senate shall have the sole power to try all impeachments. When sitting for that purpose, they shall be on oath or affirmation. When the President

Explanations and Comments

Section 3 deals exclusively with the Senate.

Senators are now elected directly by the people, a change brought about by the 17th Amendment, ratified in 1913.

Again, the word "inhabitant" instead of "legal resident" or "registered voter."

Senators, serving as jurors, must take an oath similar to that taken by any juror to perform their task honestly and to the best of their ability. The Senate's authority here is much the same as that of a court.

Answer frame 1[4]

1. True. The stated purposes are to form a more perfect union (than did the Articles of Confederation), establish justice, insure domestic tranquility, provide for the common defence, promote the general welfare, and secure the blessings of liberty to ourselves and our posterity.
2. False. Legislative powers are vested in the *Congress* of the United States, which consists of the Senate and the House of Representatives.
3. True. These are the qualifications of a Representative of the House. Each state has at least one Representative, but beyond this requirement the number of Representatives shall not exceed one for every 30,000 people.
4. False. The House does select its leaders *and* has the sole power to call these leaders to trial through the impeachment procedure. The person is tried by the Senate and a two thirds vote is necessary for removal from office.

If you missed any of the above, reread Frame 1[4] before beginning Frame 2[4] on page 25.

Frame 2[4] continued

THE CONSTITUTION (cont.)

of the United States is tried, the Chief Justice shall preside: And no person shall be convicted without the concurrence of two thirds of the members present.

Judgment in case of impeachment.—7. Judgment in cases of impeachment shall not extend further than to removal from office, and disqualification to hold and enjoy any office of honor, trust, or profit under the United States: but the party convicted shall nevertheless be liable and subject to indictment, trial, judgment and punishment, according to law.

Explanations and Comments

It may force a witness to appear and it may demand answers, under threat of a contempt citation.

Thirteen men have been impeached and four convicted in the first 185 years under the Constitution. The 13 include 1 president, 1 senator, 1 secretary of war, and 10 federal judges, one of whom was a member of the Supreme Court. The four found guilty were lower court judges. In 1974 the House Judiciary Committee recommended impeachment of President Nixon on three counts. Facing almost certain impeachment and probable conviction, he resigned in August of that year.

Indicate whether each of the following statements is true or false.

_____ 1. The number of senators from each state depends on the population of the state, and they are selected for a term of two years.

_____ 2. One-third of the Senate seats are up for election during each election year.

_____ 3. A candidate for a Senate seat must be at least 30 years of age, must have been a citizen of the United States for at least nine years, and must be an inhabitant of that state for which he or she shall be chosen.

_____ 4. The vice president serves as the president of the Senate but does not vote in any circumstances.

_____ 5. The Senate has the sole power to try all impeachments, and conviction is upon concurrence of two thirds of the members *present*.

Now turn to Answer frame 2[4] on page 28 and check your responses.

Frame 3[4]

THE CONSTITUTION (cont.)
Section 4

Control of Congressional elections—1. The times, places and manner of holding elections for Senators and Representatives, shall be prescribed in each State by the Legislature thereof; but the Congress may at any time by law make or alter such regulations, except as to the places of choosing Senators.

Time for assembling of Congress—2. The Congress shall assemble at least once in every year, and such meeting shall be on the first Monday in December, unless they shall by law appoint a different day.

Section 5

Election and qualifications of members; quorum—1. Each House shall be the judge of the elections, returns and qualifications of its own members, and a majority of each shall constitute a quorum to do business; but a smaller number may adjourn from day to day, and may be authorized to compel the attendance of absent members, in such manner, and under such penalties as each House may provide.

Each House to determine its own rules—2.

Explanations and Comments

In 1845 Congress established election day as the Tuesday after the first Monday in November. Why this date? The date fell approximately one month before electors were required to gather to cast their votes for president and vice president; Tuesday was chosen instead of Monday so that people who were forced to travel a long distance would not have to start on Sunday, a day of worship. The Tuesday after the first Monday was selected to guard against an election day falling on the first of the month—a courtesy to business interests. Why did Congress establish a national election day? With different election days in different states, it was not uncommon for politicians to transport wagonloads of men across state lines to cast ballots in key districts. Also, news of the vote in one state tended to influence the balloting in other states.

For the first 53 years of the Constitution, a voter cast ballots for as many representatives as his state was assigned. Under such a system, many sparsely populated areas were denied any representation. In 1842 Congress ordered that states be divided into Congressional Districts and that the people from each District elect one man as their representative in the House.

Here, the Founding Fathers carefully guarded against an abuse practiced by English kings, who often tried to rule without Parliament. Charles I's 11 years of "personal rule" (1629–40) brought him to the brink of the Civil War which cost him his head. Charles' father, James I, ruled for 10 years during which only one Parliament—the "Addled Parliament"—met for only a few days and was dismissed by the king. The time of assembling was changed by the 20th Amendment.

Constitutional scholars are not at all certain that a

Answer frame 2⁴

1. False. Each state has two senators regardless of population, and their term of office is six years. At first they were selected by their state legislatures, but under the 17th Amendment (ratified in 1913) they are now elected by the people.
2. True. Every two years (on even numbered years) elections are held to fill one third of the seats in the Senate and all of the seats in the House.
3. True. These are the qualifications to run for the Senate.
4. False. The vice president, as president of the Senate, votes only when the Senate is equally divided on an issue. He has the tie breaking vote.
5. True. And when impeachment occurs the result shall be no greater than removal from office and disqualification to hold and enjoy any office of honor, trust, or profit under the United States. But the person convicted is liable and subject to indictment, trial, judgment, and punishment, according to Law but not as a part of the impeachment proceeding.

If you missed any of the above, reread Frame 2⁴ before beginning Frame 3⁴ on page 27.

Frame 3⁴ continued

THE CONSTITUTION (cont.)

Each House may determine the rules of its proceedings, punish its members for disorderly behavior, and, with the concurrence of two thirds, expel a member.

Journals and yeas and nays—3. Each House shall keep a journal of its proceedings, and from time to time publish the same, excepting such parts as may in their judgment require secrecy; and the yeas and nays of the members of either House on any question shall, at the desire of one fifth of those present, be entered on the journal.

Adjournment—4. Neither House, during the session of Congress, shall, without the consent of the other, adjourn for more than three days, nor to any other place than that in which the two Houses shall be sitting.

Explanations and Comments

member of Congress may be impeached. Senator Blount was impeached in 1798 but resigned before the case came to trial in the Senate. This is the only impeachment in Congressional history and the ruling at that time—that the Senate did not have jurisdiction—has never again been tested.

Two notable instances in which the Congress punished its own members occurred in recent times: In December 1954, the Senate formally condemned Senator Joseph McCarthy (Rep., Wis.) for conduct "contrary to Senate traditions." In 1967 the House excluded Adam Clayton Powell (Dem., N.Y.), alleging he had made improper expenditures of public funds for private purposes. In a special election the following year, Powell's Harlem constituents overwhelmingly returned him to office. Although seated, he was deprived of his seniority and fined $25,000. In June 1969, the Supreme Court ruled that the House had unconstitutionally excluded Powell.

Is each of the following statements true or false?

_____ 1. Congress does not establish all of the rules for the conduct of Congressional elections.

_____ 2. There are sanctions which can be taken by a House against its members for their behavior.

_____ 3. Not all proceedings and votes by members of each House need be contained in the public record.

_____ 4. Each House, during a session of Congress, shall have sole discretion over adjournments and where it shall meet.

Now turn to Answer frame 3⁴ on page 30 and check your responses.

Frame 4⁴

THE CONSTITUTION (cont.)
SECTION 6

Compensation and privileges of Members of Congress—1. The Senators and Representatives shall receive a compensation for their services, to be ascertained by law, and paid out of the Treasury of the United States. They shall in all cases, except treason, felony and breach of the peace, be privileged from arrest during their attendance at the session of their respective Houses, and in going to and returning from the same; and for any speech or debate in either House, they shall not be questioned in any other place.

Incompatible offices—2. No Senator or Representative shall, during the time for which he was elected, be appointed to any civil office under the authority of the United States, which shall have been created, or the emoluments whereof shall have been increased during such time; and no person holding any office under the United States, shall be a member of either House during his continuance in office.

SECTION 7

Revenue bills—1. All bills for raising revenue shall originate in the House of Representatives; but the Senate may propose or concur with amendments as on other bills.

Manner of passing bills; veto power of President—2. Every bill which shall have passed the House of Representatives and the Senate, shall before it becomes a law, be presented to the President of the United States; If he approves he shall sign it, but if not he shall return it, with his objections to that House in which it shall

Explanations and Comments

Salary: $42,500—the same in both houses. The president pro tempore of Senate and the majority and minority leaders of both houses receive $7,000 additional. Speaker of the House: $62,500. President pro temporare of Senate (when there is no vice president): $62,500.

This is known as the presidential veto (literally "I forbid") power.

Answer frame 3⁴

1. True. The state legislatures prescribe the times, places, and manner of holding elections for senators and representatives. Congress may at any time by law make or alter these regulations, except as to the places for voting on senators.
2. True. Each House may punish its members for disorderly behavior and, by a two thirds vote, expel a member.
3. True. Parts of the proceedings may require secrecy and therefore not be made public. Also, the votes by members on any question are entered in the public record only if this is the desire of at least one fifth of those present.
4. False. Each House must have the consent of the other if it intends to adjourn for more than three days or to meet in any other place than that in which the two Houses shall be sitting.

If you missed any of the above, reread Frame 3⁴ before beginning Frame 4⁴ on page 29.

Frame 4⁴ continued

THE CONSTITUTION (cont.)

have originated, who shall enter the objections at large on their journal, and proceed to reconsider it. If after such reconsideration two thirds of that House shall agree to pass the bill, it shall be sent, together with the objections, to the other House, by which it shall likewise be reconsidered, and if approved by two thirds of that House, it shall become a law. But in all such Cases the Votes of both Houses shall be determined by yeas and nays, and the names of the persons voting for and against the bill shall be entered on the journal of each House respectively. If any bill shall not be returned by the President within ten days (Sundays excepted) after it shall have been presented to him, the same shall be a law, in like manner as if he had signed it, unless the Congress by their adjournment prevent its return, in which case it shall not be a Law.

Explanations and Comments

Consider what a powerful tool the presidential veto is! If the president says "I forbid," both houses must pass the bill by a two-thirds vote instead of by a simple majority.

The Reorganization Act of 1970 approved voting by electronic method in the House and the system was installed and placed in operation with the beginning of the 93rd Congress in January 1973.

This withholding is known as a "pocket veto." The pocket veto is often employed by presidents when a great number of bills are rushed to them in the closing days of the session. Rather than write long and hasty objections, presidents "put the bills in their pockets" and thus prevent passage.

(Some state constitutions, particularly the more modern ones, have provisions by which the governor may veto parts of a bill. The U.S. Constitution has no such provision: a veto of any part constitutes a veto of the whole. Statistics dramatically prove the power of the veto: through the adjournment of the 92nd Congress in 1972, Congress overrode the presidential veto only 77 times. Andrew Johnson was overridden most often—15 times; Presidents Tyler, Hayes, Arthur, Benjamin Harrison, Theodore Roosevelt, and Taft each suffered only a single override; Richard Nixon's last full session (the 92nd) found him overturned only twice.) Four men, Cleveland, with 584 vetoes (and 7 overrides), Truman, 250 (12), Eisenhower, 181 (2), and Franklin Roosevelt, 631 (9), accounted for 1,646 of the approximately 2,300 vetoes in American History through the Nixon resignation. Most of Cleveland's vetoes concerned small, private pensions. At the other extreme, Adams and Jefferson did not exercise the veto power once in their 12 years.

THE CONSTITUTION (cont.)

Concurrent orders or resolutions—3. Every order, resolution, or vote to which the concurrence of the Senate and House of Representatives may be necessary (except on a question of adjournment) shall be presented to the President of the United States; and before the same shall take effect, shall be approved by him, or being disapproved by him, shall be repassed by two thirds of the Senate and House of Representatives, according to the rule and limitations prescribed in the case of a bill.

True or false?

_____ 1. Senators and representatives cannot be arrested for a minor traffic violation while going to or returning from a session of their House.

_____ 2. Senators and representatives cannot be held legally liable for anything they say on the floor of the House or the Senate.

_____ 3. All bills for raising revenue shall originate in the Senate.

_____ 4. If the president vetoes a bill it may still become law.

_____ 5. If any bill is not returned by the president within ten days (Sundays excepted) after it has been presented to him, it shall be considered to be vetoed.

Now turn to Answer frame 4[4] on page 32 and check your responses.

Frame 5[4]

THE CONSTITUTION (cont.)	**Explanations and Comments**

SECTION 8

The Congress shall have Power

Taxes—1. To lay and collect taxes, duties, imposts and excises, to pay the debts and provide for the common defence and general welfare of the United States; but all duties, imposts and excises shall be uniform throughout the United States.

These are the so-called "enumerated" powers of the Congress.

Borrowing—2. To borrow money on the credit of the United States.

Regulation of commerce—3. To regulate commerce with foreign nations, and among the several States, and with the Indian tribes.

This is the powerful "commerce clause" which Congress and the courts have currently interpreted as giving the Congress almost unlimited power to regulate business. It is difficult to conceive of a business transaction, no matter how local in concept, that cannot be interpreted as coming under "interstate commerce."

Naturalization and bankruptcy—4. To establish a uniform rule of naturalization, and uniform laws on the subject of bankruptcies throughout the United States.

Money, weights and measures—5. To coin money, regulate the value thereof, and of foreign coin, and fix the standard of weights and measures.

Answer frame 4⁴

1. True. They can only be arrested for treason, felony, or breach of the peace during their attendance at a session of their House, and in going to and returning from the same.
2. True. They shall not be questioned in any other place for any speech or debate in either House.
3. False. All such bills shall originate in the *House*.
4. True. If it receives a two thirds affirmative vote in both the House and Senate after it is reconsidered it becomes law. The names of the persons voting for and against the bill are recorded in the journal of each House.
5. False. Under these circumstances it shall be a law as if he had signed it unless Congress by their adjournment prevents its return.

If you missed any of the above, reread Frame 4⁴ before beginning Frame 5⁴ on page 31.

Frame 5⁴ continued

THE CONSTITUTION (cont.)

Counterfeiting—6. To provide for the punishment of counterfeiting the securities and current coin of the United States.

Post offices—7. To establish post offices and post roads.

Patents and copyrights—8. To promote the progress of science and useful arts, by securing for limited times to authors and inventors the exclusive right to their respective writings and discoveries.

Inferior courts—9. To constitute tribunals inferior to the Supreme Court.

Piracies and felonies—10. To define and punish piracies and felonies committed on the high seas, and offenses against the law of nations.

War—11. To declare war, grant letters of marque and reprisal, and make rules concerning captures on land and water.

Armies—12. To raise and support armies, but no appropriation of money to that use shall be for a longer term than two years.

Navy—13. To provide and maintain a navy.

Land and naval forces—14. To make rules for the government and regulation of the land and naval forces.

Calling out militia—15. To provide for calling forth the militia to execute the laws of the Union, suppress insurrections and repel invasions.

Organizing, arming and disciplining militia —16. To provide for organizing, arming, and disciplining the militia, and for governing such part of them as may be employed in the service of the United States, reserving to the States, respectively, the appointment of the officers, and

THE CONSTITUTION (cont.)	**Explanations and Comments**

the authority of training the militia according to the discipline prescribed by Congress.

District of Columbia—17. To exercise exclusive legislation in all cases whatsoever, over such district (not exceeding ten miles square) as may, by cession of particular states, and the acceptance of Congress, become the seat of the Government of the United States, and to exercise like authority over all places purchased by the consent of the Legislature of the State in which the same shall be, for the erection of forts, magazines, arsenals, dockyards, and other needful buildings;—And

To enact laws necessary to enforce Constitution—18. To make all laws which shall be necessary and proper for carrying into execution the foregoing powers, and all other powers vested by this Constitution in the Government of the United States, or in any department or office thereof.

This is the famous "necessary and proper" clause, the fountain from which many of the *assumed* powers of Congress flows. Its current interpretation is vigorously protested by states' righters.

Indicate whether each of the following statements is true or false.

_____ 1.   Congress can levy one level of excise tax on the West Coast and a different level of the same excise tax on the East Coast in order to achieve national goals.

_____ 2.   Congress has the authority to regulate commerce with foreign nations but not among the states.

_____ 3.   Congress has broad powers over money and national security.

_____ 4.   Not every city in the United States is contained within a state.

Now turn to Answer frame 5[4] on page 34 and check your responses.

Frame 6[4]

THE CONSTITUTION (cont.)	**Explanations and Comments**
SECTION 9	

Slave trade—1. The migration or importation of such persons as any of the States now existing shall think proper to admit, shall not be prohibited by the Congress prior to the year one thousand eight hundred and eight, but a tax or duty may be imposed on such importation, not exceeding ten dollars for each person.

Writ of habeas corpus—2. The privilege of the writ of habeas corpus shall not be suspended, unless when in cases of rebellion or invasion the public safety may require it.

Bills of attainder and ex post facto laws prohibited—3. No bill of attainder or ex post facto law shall be passed.

This section contains prohibitions on the Congress.

Answer frame 5⁴ _____

1. False. All duties, imposts, and excises must be uniform throughout the United States.
2. False. It has power to regulate commerce with foreign nations *and* among the several states (and with the Indian tribes—not very relevant now).
3. True. It can coin, borrow, and punish counterfeiting of money. It also can raise, support, and regulate military forces, declare war, and call out the militia.
4. True. Washington, D.C., is not contained within a state but is instead under the direct jurisdiction of Congress.

If you missed any of the above, reread Frame 5⁴ before beginning Frame 6⁴ on page 33.

Frame 6⁴ continued

THE CONSTITUTION (cont.)

Capitation and other direct taxes—4. No capitation, or other direct tax shall be laid, unless in proportion to the census or enumeration herein before directed to be taken.

Exports not to be taxed—5. No tax or duty shall be laid on articles exported from any State.

Shipping—6. No preference shall be given by any regulation of commerce or revenue to the ports of one State over those of another; nor shall vessels bound to, or from, one State, be obliged to enter, clear, or pay duties in another.

Appropriations; reports—7. No money shall be drawn from the Treasury, but in consequence of appropriations made by law; and a regular statement and account of the receipts and expenditures of all public money shall be published from time to time.

Titles of nobility; favors from foreign powers—8. No title of nobility shall be granted by the United States: And no person holding any office of profit or trust under them, shall without the consent of the Congress, accept of any present, emolument, office, or title, of any kind whatever, from any king, prince, or foreign state.

Indicate whether each of the following statements is true or false by writing "T" or "F" in the space provided.

_____ 1. From its inception Congress has had the power to ban slave trade.

_____ 2. There are certain instances in which the writ of habeas corpus (the right to a speedy trial) shall be suspended.

_____ 3. The Constitution had certain provisions to promote free trade between the states.

_____ 4. The United States government may grant titles of nobility.

Now turn to Answer frame 6⁴ on page 36 and check your responses.

Frame 7⁴

THE CONSTITUTION (cont.)
SECTION 10

Limitations of the powers of the several States
—1. No State shall enter into any treaty, alliance, or confederation; grant letters of marque and reprisal; coin money; emit bills of credit; make anything but gold and silver coin a tender in payment of debts; pass any bill of attainder, ex post facto law, or law impairing the obligation of contracts or grant any title of nobility.

State imposts and duties—2. No State shall, without the consent of the Congress, lay any imposts or duties on imports or exports, except what may be absolutely necessary for executing its inspection laws; and the net produce of all duties and imposts, laid by any State on imports or exports, shall be for the use of the Treasury of the United States; and all such laws shall be subject to the revision and control of the Congress.

Further restrictions on powers of States—3. No State shall, without the consent of Congress, lay any duty of tonnage, keep troops, or ships of war in time of peace, enter into any agreement or compact with another State, or with a foreign power, or engage in war, unless actually invaded, or in such imminent danger as will not admit of delay.

Explanations and Comments

This section contains prohibitions on the states. Students should be particularly careful not to confuse the prohibitions on the Congress (Sec. 9) with the prohibitions on the States (Sec. 10). *This is one of the foremost traps in constitutional examinations!*

Indicate whether each of the following statements is true or false by writing "T" or "F" in the space provided.

_____ 1. States have the right to enter into a treaty.

_____ 2. If a state has the consent of Congress and imposes a duty on imports and exports the net proceeds of such duty will be for its own use.

_____ 3. A state may not keep troops in time of peace without consent of Congress.

_____ 4. A state may engage in war without the consent of Congress but only in very dire circumstances.

Now turn to Answer frame 7⁴ on page 36 and check your responses.

Answer frame 6[4]

1. False. Congress was not given this authority immediately. The Constitution specified 1808 as the year in which this power became effective.
2. True. In cases of rebellion or invasion the public safety may require its suspension.
3. True. Two such provisions were the one which prevents exports from any state to be taxed and the provision which prohibits preference to the ports of one state over another and the payment of duties by one state to another.
4. False. It may not, and neither may any person holding any office in the government accept (without the consent of Congress) any such designation from any king, prince, or foreign state.

If you missed any of the above, reread Frame 6[4] before beginning Frame 7[4] on page 35.

Answer frame 7[4]

1. False. They are prohibited from entering into any treaty, alliance, or confederation.
2. False. They shall be for the use of the Treasury of the United States.
3. True. States are prohibited from keeping troops or ships of war in time of peace without the consent of Congress.
4. True. Only if a state is actually invaded or is in such imminent danger that no delay is feasible may it engage in war.

If you missed any of the above, reread Frame 7[4] before beginning Frame 8[4] on page 35.

Frame 8[4]

THE CONSTITUTION (cont.)
ARTICLE TWO

SECTION 1

The President; the executive power—1. The Executive power shall be vested in a President of the United States of America. He shall hold his office during the term of four years, and, together with the Vice President, chosen for the same term, be elected, as follows:

Appointment and qualifications of presidential electors—2. Each State shall appoint, in such manner as the legislature thereof may direct, a number of electors, equal to the whole number of Senators and Representatives to which the State may be entitled in the Congress; but no Senator or Representative or person holding an office of trust or profit under the United States, shall be appointed an elector.

Original method of electing the President and Vice-President [The electors shall meet in their respective States, and vote by ballot for two persons, of whom one at least shall not be an inhabitant of the same state with themselves. And they shall make a list of all the persons voted for, and of the number of votes for each; which list they shall sign and certify, and trans-

Explanations and Comments
ARTICLE TWO—The Executive

Overturned by the 12th Amendment, which was prompted by the political fiasco in which Aaron Burr almost stole the presidency from Thomas Jefferson following the election of 1800. For further discussion, see commentary on the 12th Amendment.

THE CONSTITUTION (cont.)

mit sealed to the seat of the Government of the United States, directed to the President of the Senate. The President of the Senate shall, in the presence of the Senate and House of Representatives, open all the certificates, and the votes shall then be counted. The person having the greatest number of votes shall be the President, if such number be a majority of the whole number of electors appointed; and if there be more than one who have such majority, and have an equal number of votes, then the House of Representatives shall immediately choose by ballot one of them for President; and if no person have a majority, then from the five highest on the list the said House shall in like manner choose the President. But in choosing the President, the votes shall be taken by States, the representation from each State having one vote; a quorum for this purpose shall consist of a member or members from two thirds of the States, and a majority of all the States shall be necessary to a choice. In every case, after the choice of the President, the person having the greatest number of votes of the electors shall be the Vice President. But if there should remain two or more who have equal votes, the Senate shall choose from them by ballot the Vice President.]

Electors—3. The Congress may determine the time of choosing the electors, and the day on which they shall give their votes; which day shall be the same throughout the United States.

Qualifications for President—4. No person except a natural born citizen, or a citizen of the United States, at the time of the adoption of this Constitution, shall be eligible to the office of President; neither shall any person be eligible to that office who shall not have attained to the age of thirty-five years, and been fourteen years a resident within the United States.

Filling vacancy in the office of President—5. In case of the removal of the President from office, or of his death, resignation, or inability to discharge the powers and duties of the said office, the same shall devolve on the Vice President, and the Congress may by law provide for the case of removal, death, resignation or inability, both of the President and Vice President, declaring what officer shall then act as President, and such officer shall act accordingly, until the

Explanations and Comments

First Tuesday after the first Monday in November. Electors "give their votes" on the Monday following the second Wednesday in December.

This ruled out Alexander Hamilton, born a British subject on the island of Nevis in the West Indies. Because of this clause, Henry Kissinger could become president only by constitutional amendment.

This was one of the most controversial clauses in the Constitution. The phrase "inability to discharge the powers and duties" was especially relevant during the second administration of Woodrow Wilson. Presidents Eisenhower and Lyndon B. Johnson also suffered periods of disability.

The question of whether a vice president became a full-fledged president upon succeeding to the presidency first arose when John Tyler succeeded President William Henry Harrison in 1841. Tyler as-

THE CONSTITUTION (cont.)

disability be removed, or a President shall be elected.

Compensation of the President—6. The President shall, at stated times, receive for his services, a compensation, which shall neither be increased nor diminished during the period for which he shall have been elected, and he shall not receive within that period any other emolument from the United States, or any of them.

Oath to be taken by the President—7. Before he enter on the execution of his office, he shall take the following oath or affirmation:—"I do solemnly swear (or affirm) that I will faithfully execute the office of President of the United States, and will to the best of my ability, preserve, protect and defend the Constitution of the United States."

Explanations and Comments

sumed that the Constitution clothed him with all the authority of a duly-elected president, and the precedent thus established has never been questioned.

The 25th Amendment has established a new line of succession and cleared up the ambiguities of Paragraph 6. See the comment on the 25th Amendment.

Annual salary: $200,000 (1974), the vice president receives $62,500.

Indicate whether each of the following statements is true or false by writing "T" or "F" in the space provided.

_____ 1.   The president is elected directly by the people.

_____ 2.   A person must be a natural born citizen (born in the United States) to become president.

_____ 3.   The president's salary may be increased or decreased while that person is in office.

_____ 4.   The president must take an oath before beginning to serve in that office.

Now turn to Answer frame 8[4] on page 40 and check your responses.

Frame 9[4]

THE CONSTITUTION (cont.)
SECTION 2

The President to be commander-in-chief and head of executive department; reprieves and pardons—1. The President shall be Commander-in-Chief of the Army and Navy of the United States, and of the militia of the several States, when called into the actual service of the United States; he may require the opinion, in writing, of the principal officer in each of the executive departments, upon any subject relating to the duties of their respective offices, and he shall

Explanations and Comments

All three paragraphs of Section 2 deal with the powers of the president. Note that the reprieve and pardon powers extend only to offenses in *federal* cases.

THE CONSTITUTION (cont.)	Explanations and Comments

have power to grant reprieves and pardons for offenses against the United States, except in cases of impeachment.

Treaties; ambassadors; inferior officers—2. He shall have power, by and with the advice and consent of the Senate to make treaties, provided two thirds of the Senators present concur; and he shall nominate, and by and with the advice and consent of the Senate, shall appoint ambassadors, other public ministers and consuls, judges of the Supreme Court, and all other officers of the United States, whose appointments are not herein otherwise provided for, and which shall be established by law; but the Congress may by law vest the appointment of such inferior officers, as they think proper, in the President alone, in the courts of law, or in the heads of departments.

President may fill vacancies in office during recess of Senate—3. The President shall have the power to fill all vacancies that may happen during the recess of the Senate, by granting commissions, which shall expire at the end of their next session.

SECTION 3

President to give advice to Congress; may convene or adjourn it on certain occasions; to receive ambassadors, etc.; have laws executed and commission all officers—He shall from time to time give to the Congress information of the state of the Union, and recommend to their consideration such measures as he shall judge necessary and expedient; he may, on extraordinary occasions, convene both Houses, or either of them, and in case of disagreement between them, with respect to the time of adjournment, he may adjourn them to such time as he shall think proper; he shall receive ambassadors and other public ministers; he shall take care that the laws be faithfully executed, and shall commission all the officers of the United States.

Section 3 spells out the required duties of the president.

The president has the option of delivering the state of the union address before a joint session of the Congress, or of sending the message to be read. Most modern presidents have delivered the address in person, in the full glare of coverage by all the major television and radio networks. The state of the union message is one of the first orders of business in every new Congress; another important speech is the budget message.

No president has ever adjourned Congress.

SECTION 4

All civil officers removable by impeachment—The President, Vice President, and all civil officers of the United States, shall be removed from office on impeachment for, and conviction of, treason, bribery, or other high crimes and misdemeanors.

The definition of "other high crimes and misdemeanors" has never been satisfactorily settled. Only the Senate, sitting as a court of impeachment, can make this determination. There is no appeal from an impeachment conviction, not even to the Supreme Court.

Answer frame 8⁴

1. False. Technically, the president is elected by electors appointed by each State. This group is known as the "electoral college."
2. True. And he or she must also be at least 35 years of age and must have resided in the United States for at least 14 years.
3. False. The president's salary may not be changed while that person is in office. Salary changes enacted during that period would apply to the next person filling that office.
4. True. The oath he or she must take is, "I do solemnly swear (or affirm) that I will faithfully execute the office of the President of the United States, and will to the best of my ability, preserve, protect and defend the Constitution of the United States."

If you missed any of the above, reread Frame 8⁴ before beginning Frame 9⁴ on page 38.

Frame 9⁴ continued

Indicate whether each of the following statements is true or false.

_____ 1. The chairman of the Joint Chiefs of Staff is the commander in chief of the Army and Navy of the United States.

_____ 2. The president has the sole power to make treaties and place ambassadors and judges of the Supreme Court in their respective positions.

_____ 3. The president has the power to convene or adjourn the Congress on certain occasions.

_____ 4. The president or any other civil officer of the United States may be removed from office on impeachment for and conviction of any crime.

Now turn to Answer frame 9⁴ on page 42 and check your responses.

Frame 10⁴

THE CONSTITUTION (cont.)
ARTICLE THREE

SECTION 1

Judicial power; term of office and compensation of judges—The judicial power of the United States shall be vested in one Supreme Court, and in such inferior courts as the Congress may from time to time ordain and establish. The judges, both of the Supreme and inferior courts, shall hold their offices during good behavior, and shall, at stated times, receive for their services a compensation which shall not be diminished during their continuance in office.

Explanations and Comments
ARTICLE THREE—The Judiciary

Article Three merely establishes a Supreme Court, sketches in the judicial purview, and defines treason. The details are left to the Congress.

The Judiciary Act of 1789 established a Supreme Court of one chief justice and five associate justices; it further created 13 federal district courts of one justice each and three circuit courts, each consisting of one district court justice sitting with two Supreme Court justices. The Act went on to specify the jurisdiction and organization of the federal courts. State courts, granted concurrent jurisdiction in instances where federal law was being adjudicated, were in effect incorporated into the federal system. Justices of all state courts are bound by oaths to the *federal* as well as the state constitution (Article Six).

THE CONSTITUTION (cont.)

Explanations and Comments

Associate justices receive an annual salary of $60,-000; the chief justice receives $62,500; the circuit judges receive $42,500 (1974).

It is easy to see the necessity for the clause which forbids pay reductions. Otherwise Congress, which sets federal court salaries, could conceivably control the justices' votes by threatening to reduce their wages.

SECTION 2

Jurisdiction of Federal courts—1. The judicial power shall extend to all cases, in law and equity, arising under this Constitution, the laws of the United States, and treaties made, or which shall be made, under their authority; to all cases affecting ambassadors, other public ministers and consuls; to all cases of admiralty and maritime jurisdiction; to controversies to which the United States shall be a party; to controversies between two or more States; between a State and citizens of another State; between citizens of different States; between citizens of the same State claiming lands under grants of different States [and between a State, or the citizens thereof, and foreign states, citizens, or subjects.]

This section was abridged by the 11th Amendment.

Original and appellate jurisdiction of Supreme Court—2. In all cases affecting ambassadors, other public ministers and consuls, and those in which a State shall be party, the Supreme Court shall have original jurisdiction. In all the other cases before mentioned, the Supreme Court shall have appellate jurisdiction, both as to law and fact, with such exceptions, and under such regulations as the Congress shall make.

Trial of all crimes, except impeachment, to be by jury—3. The trial of all crimes, except in cases of impeachment, shall be by jury; and such trial shall be held in the State where the said crimes shall have been committed; but when not committed within any State, the trial shall be at such place or places as the Congress may by law have directed.

SECTION 3

Treason defined; conviction of—1. Treason against the United States, shall consist only in levying war against them, or, in adhering to their enemies, giving them aid and comfort. No per-

Answer frame 9⁴

1. False. The *president* is the commander-in-chief of the Army and Navy of the United States.
2. False. He must have the advice and consent of the Senate to do these things. Treaties must be approved by two thirds of the senators present.
3. True. On extraordinary occasions the president may convene one or both Houses. And in case they cannot agree on a time of adjournment, the president may adjourn them.
4. False. The Constitution says that removal from office may result on impeachment for and conviction of treason, bribery, or other high crimes and misdemeanors. The exact meaning of these terms is subject to debate.

If you missed any of the above, reread Frame 9⁴ before beginning Frame 10⁴ on page 40.

Frame 10⁴ continued

THE CONSTITUTION (cont.)

son shall be convicted of treason unless on the testimony of two witnesses to the same overt act, or on confession in open court.

Congress to declare punishment for treason —2. The Congress shall have power to declare the punishment of treason, but no attainder of treason shall work corruption of blood, or forfeiture except during the life of the person attained.

True or false?

———— 1. Aside from the establishment of a Supreme Court, Congress was given the power by the Constitution to determine the details of the court structure in the United States.

———— 2. In most cases before it, the Supreme Court acts as a court of appeals (reviews cases that have already been tried in a lower court).

———— 3. A jury trial is required for all crimes, and the trial is held in the state where the crime was committed.

———— 4. A person cannot be convicted of treason unless there is testimony against him of two witnesses to the same overt act.

Now turn to Answer frame 10⁴ on page 44 and check your responses.

Frame 11⁴

THE CONSTITUTION (cont.)
ARTICLE FOUR
SECTION 1

Each State to give full faith and credit to the public acts and records of other States—Full faith and credit shall be given in each State to

Explanations and Comments
ARTICLE FOUR—Full faith and credit

Imagine the chaos which would follow if the marriages, divorces, and contracts executed in Georgia were not recognized in Alabama (or Wisconsin,

THE CONSTITUTION (cont.)

the public acts, records, and judicial proceedings of every other State. And the Congress may by general laws prescribe the manner in which such acts, records and proceedings shall be proved, and the effect thereof.

Explanations and Comments

Maine, or Utah)! Article Four guards against this possibility. The term "judicial proceedings" takes in all state laws and decrees. In some instances, a state may set certain minimum qualifications for its acceptance of decrees of other states.

Professional licenses, being neither state laws nor edicts of a court, do not fall under the full faith and credit umbrella. Recognized state licensing and accrediting associations are free to set their own qualifications and to decide whether to make reciprocal arrangements with agencies in other states. Thus Florida could guard against a winter influx of thousands of barbers (or beauty operators, lawyers, doctors, or CPAs) who might conceivably starve the resident professional workers and taxpayers.

Note that full faith and credit regulations *apply only to the states*. There is no reference to the public acts, and so on, of other countries.

SECTION 2

Privileges of citizens–1. The citizens of each state shall be entitled to all privileges and immunities of citizens in the several States.

This assures fair treatment for visitors, traveling salesmen, out of state students, and servicemen, and so on.

Extradition between the several States–2. A person charged in any State with treason, felony, or other crime, who shall flee from justice, and be found in another State, shall on the demand of the executive authority of the State from which he fled, be delivered up, to be removed to the State having jurisdiction of the crime.

Without this clause a state might accept bribes, create a haven for fugitive criminals, and thwart the orderly criminal procedure of the nation.

Slaves–3. No person held to service or labor in one State under the laws thereof, escaping into another, shall, in consequence of any law or regulation therein, be discharged from such service or labor, but shall be delivered up on claim of the party to whom such service or labor may be due.

Outdated by the 13th Amendment, ratified in 1865. See comment on the Dred Scott decision in Chapter 6 on page 73.

SECTION 3

New States–1. New States may be admitted by the Congress into this Union; but no new State shall be formed or erected within the jurisdiction of any other State; nor any State be formed by junction of two or more States, or parts of States, without the consent of the Legislatures of the States concerned as well as of the Congress.

Although Congress controls the admission of new states, note that states already in the Union are assured of their lands by the clause which requires their consent on any change of ownership.

Regulations concerning territory–2. The Congress shall have power to dispose of and make all needful rules and regulations respecting the territory or other property belonging to the

Again, as in paragraph 1, it is the *Congress* which is vested with the power to admit new states and make regulations concerning them. Although several presidents, notably Polk, were vigorous in such

Answer frame 10⁴

1. True. Congress was vested with this power. And since the Constitution was silent as to the number of justices on the Supreme Court they even had to determine this.
2. True. The Supreme Court has *original* jurisdiction only in cases involving ambassadors, other public ministers and consuls, and those in which a state is a party. Most of the cases coming before the Court involve appeals of lower court decisions.
3. False. All crimes *except impeachment* require a jury trial. A trial for a president who has been impeached would be held in the Senate, with the chief justice of the Supreme Court presiding. Other crimes are tried in the state where they were committed.
4. False. He may also be convicted of treason if he confesses in open court.

If you missed any of the above, reread Frame 10⁴ before beginning Frame 11⁴ on page 42.

Frame 11⁴ continued

THE CONSTITUTION (cont.)

United States; and nothing in this Constitution shall be so construed as to prejudice any claims of the United States, or of any particular State.

SECTION 4

Republican form of government and protection guaranteed the several States—The United States shall guarantee to every State in this Union a Republican form of government, and shall protect each of them against invasion; and on application of the Legislature, or of the Executive (when the Legislature cannot be convened) against domestic violence.

Explanations and Comments

promotions, they were legally without power to act and totally subject to the views of Congress.

A "Republican form of government" might be defined as one operated by properly representative delegates freely elected by the people. It would prohibit rule in any of the states by any king, emperor, dynasty, or hereditary ruler.

Indicate whether each of the following statements is true or false by writing "T" or "F" in the space provided.

_____ 1. The Constitution requires that each state respect the actions and proceedings of every other state.

_____ 2. A person committing a crime in one state and fleeing to another may be apprehended and must be returned to the state in which the crime was committed if that state so demands.

_____ 3. Congress has the sole authority to approve new states which are formed within an existing state or by a combination of two or more existing states.

_____ 4. Each of the states is guaranteed protection against invasion under the Constitution.

Now turn to Answer frame 11⁴ on page 46 and check your responses.

Frame 12[4]

THE CONSTITUTION (cont.)
ARTICLE FIVE

Ways in which the Constitution can be amended—The Congress, whenever two thirds of both Houses shall deem it necessary, shall propose amendments to this Constitution, or, on the application of the Legislatures of two thirds of the several States, shall call a convention for proposing amendments, which, in either case, shall be valid to all intents and purposes, as part of this Constitution, when ratified by the Legislatures of three fourths of the several States, or by conventions in three fourths thereof, as the one or the other mode of ratification may be proposed by the Congress; provided that no amendment which may be made prior to the year one thousand eight hundred and eight shall in any manner affect the first and fourth clauses in the Ninth Section of the First Article; and that no State, without its consent, shall be deprived of its equal suffrage in the Senate.

Explanations and Comments
ARTICLE FIVE—The Amending Article

No amendment has ever been proposed by the state legislatures.

Twenty-five of the first 26 amendments were ratified by state legislatures.

The 21st Amendment was ratified by the convention method.

Although Article Five contains no such recommendation, most proposed Amendments prescribe a time limit for ratification.

Since there is no Constitutional restriction, state legislatures which have ratified an amendment have later tried to change their minds and voted to reject the same amendment. This has happened, for instance, in the case of the proposed 27th Amendment calling for equal rights for women. This is probably illegal—see discussion in Chapter 5 on amendments.

Presidents have often actively campaigned for and against amendments. But note especially that Article Five vests the amending power in the Congress and in the state legislatures—two legislative bodies. The president has absolutely no legal power in the amending process.

For further information on the amending process and on the individual amendments, see Chapter 5.

ARTICLE SIX

ARTICLE SIX

Article Six exudes the strength and vigor and personality of the new nation. It is the authority which breathes Constitutional oxygen into all the other articles and the amendments. It seeks to establish honor and credit in the family of nations, and on the home front it binds both federal and state officials to a solemn oath of allegiance.

Debts contracted under the Confederation secured—1. All debts contracted and engagements entered into, before the adoption of this Constitution, shall be as valid against the United States under this Constitution, as under the Confederation.

This paragraph tells the world "Do not worry, we will honor all our just debts," (which were in excess of $80 million. Once these debts were paid, of course, this paragraph became obsolete).

Constitution, laws and treaties of the United States to be supreme—2. This Constitution, and the laws of the United States which shall be

Paragraph 2 establishes the Constitution, the laws of the U.S., and treaties as the "supreme law of the land," binds every judge to this solemn commit-

Answer frame 11⁴

1. True. The Constitution says that "full faith and credit shall be given in each State to the public acts, records, and judicial proceedings of every other State."
2. True. This is called extradition. On demand of the executive authority of the state from which the criminal fled after committing a crime, he must be returned. One can fight extradition on legal grounds, but unless the grounds are valid (for example, this person could not have committed the crime) extradition usually will result. Extradition is discretionary on the part of the state upon which the demand is made.
3. False. The legislatures of the state concerned must also give their consent. This provision adds stability and security to the existing states within the United States.
4. True. And at the time of ratification this was significant since Georgia in particular felt the need for such protection from the Creek Indians.

If you missed any of the above, reread Frame 11⁴ before beginning Frame 12⁴ on page 45.

Frame 12⁴ continued

THE CONSTITUTION (cont.)

made in pursuance thereof; and all treaties made, or which shall be made, under the authority of the United States, shall be the supreme law of the land; and the judges in every State shall be bound thereby, any thing in the Constitution or laws of any State to the contrary notwithstanding.

Who shall take constitutional oaths; no religious test—3. The Senators and Representatives before mentioned, and the members of the several State Legislatures, and all executive and judicial officers, both of the United States and of the several States, shall be bound by oath or affirmation, to support this Constitution; but no religious test shall ever be required as a qualification to any office or public trust under the United States.

ARTICLE SEVEN

Ratification—The ratification of the Conventions of nine States shall be sufficient for the establishment of this Constitution between the States so ratifying the same.

Done in Convention by the Unanimous Consent of the States present the Seventeenth Day of September in the Year of our Lord one thousand seven hundred and Eighty seven and of the Independence

Explanations and Comments

ment, and in precise language tells the states that they may not make laws abridging the national authority. Note that *state* judges must support the *federal* constitution.

Paragraph 3 places congressmen, members of state legislatures, and all state and national executive and judicial officials under oath to the national constitution. It also stipulates that no religious test may ever be made a requirement for public office.

ARTICLE SEVEN—The Ratification Article

Since Rhode Island had indicated opposition to the Constitution, this meant *9 out of 12*.

The new Constitution was scheduled to go into effect March 4, 1789. Although that is still usually considered the *official date*, the inauguration of President Washington was delayed until April 30.

For detailed comment on the ratification process, see Chapter 3.

THE CONSTITUTION (cont.)

of the United States of America the Twelfth. In Witness whereof We have hereunto subscribed our Names.

Gº. WASHINGTON
President and Deputy from Virginia

NEW HAMPSHIRE.

John Langdon	Nicholas Gilman

MASSACHUSETTS.

Nathaniel Gorham	Rufus King

CONNECTICUT.

Wm. Saml. Johnson	Roger Sherman

NEW YORK.

Alexander Hamilton

NEW JERSEY.

Wil: Livingston	Wm. Patterson
David Brearley	Jona: Dayton

PENNSYLVANIA.

B. Franklin	Thomas Mifflin
Robt. Morris	Geo. Clymer
Thos. Fitzsimmons	Jared Ingersoll
James Wilson	Gouv. Morris

DELAWARE.

Geo: Reed	Gunning Bedford Jun
John Dickinson	Richard Bassett
Jaco: Broom	

MARYLAND.

James McHenry	Dan: of St. Thos. Jenifer
Danl. Carroll	

VIRGINIA.

John Blair	James Madison Jr.

NORTH CAROLINA.

Wm. Blount	Richd. Dobbs Spaight
Hu. Williamson	

SOUTH CAROLINA.

J. Rutledge	Charles Cotesworth
Charles Pinckney	Pinckney
	Pierce Butler

GEORGIA.

William Few	Abr. Baldwin

Attest: WILLIAM JACKSON, *Secretary*

True or false?

_____1. Amendments to the Constitution may be made by a two thirds vote in both Houses of Congress and the signing of the measure by the president.

_____2. An amendment cannot be passed which would deprive a state of its two senators without its consent.

_____3. A federal law takes precedence over a state law if they are in conflict.

_____4. Senators and representatives, members of the state legislatures, and all executive and judicial officers must take a religious oath before assuming office.

Now turn to Answer frame 12[4] on page 50 and check your responses.

chapter 5

THE AMENDING PROCESS

Frame 1[5]

The least understood article

Gerald Ford's succession to the presidency, his nomination of Nelson Rockefeller to the vice presidency, and the grant of a full pardon to Richard Nixon: these were the highlights of the constitutionally traumatic month which began on August 9, 1974.

The sudden and bewildering series of events came in the afterglow of Mr. Nixon's admission of new Watergate coverups, the clamor for impeachment, and the resignation address carried on nationwide and satellite television. It all served to spotlight attention on Article Five, the amending article—surely one of the most misunderstood paragraphs in the American Constitution.

Mr. Ford became the first nonelected vice president in American history by the grace of Section 2 of the 25th Amendment. He had been nominated by President Nixon and confirmed by a majority vote of both Houses to fill the vacancy left by Spiro Agnew's resignation under fire.

President Ford's accession to the presidency on August 9 was provided for by Section 1 of the 25th Amendment.

And the public and journalistic yelp over the unprecedented grant of a pardon to Mr. Nixon, *prior to any conviction,* prompted numerous suggestions for constitutional amendments. For example, Senator Mondale (Dem., Minn.) swiftly suggested an amendment which would allow the Congress, by a two-thirds vote, to override a presidential pardon. There was considerable sentiment, too, for an amendment to override various parts of the 25th Amendment.

The great safety valve

The amending process is a critical one in any Constitution. It is the safety valve which corrects mistakes, permits adjustments, allows for growing pains, and provides for the final link in an elaborate series of checks and balances.

The amendment is an instrument which must be employed only after thoughtful deliberation. If alterations can be made at the whim of every articulate faction, the intent of the Founders will swiftly be undermined; if the process is too glacial, there is no way to adjust to new problems, philosophies, and technological advancements. All of the imperfections of the Articles of Confederation might have been rectified if the amending article, *which required unanimous approval of the states,* had been less rigid.

The Founding Fathers, in scrapping the Articles, were not about to box themselves into another position wherein a state with 2 percent of the population could frustrate 12 states with 98 percent of the population. They strove to create an amending process that would be both firm and flexible, one that would require careful thought and preparation over a reasonable period of time.

The record, most people will agree, shows their goals were achieved remarkably well. As these lines are being written, the American Constitution has been amended 26 times and a 27th Amendment has a reasonable chance of enactment. If the first ten amendments, known collectively as the Bill of Rights, are ruled out because they were packaged as a mere formality, the Constitution may be said to have been amended only 16 times in 185 years, or once every 11½ years. Ten of these 16 are concerned in some way with the elective process.

The amendment pattern

Constitutional amendments, like grapes, seem to come in bunches. And, just as with some fruits, there seems to be periods of drought and harvest. We have seen how the first ten amendments were adopted in a blanket measure in 1791. The period from 1791 to 1865 was constitutionally stagnant, with only two amendments being approved; then, abruptly, three "Civil War Amendments" were hustled through the Congress and the states in five years. This was followed by another drought: for 48 years not a single instance of constitutional surgery was performed. In another, now almost predictable, reversal, four amendments became law between 1913 and 1921. The years 1921 through 1933 were stand-pat, do-nothing years, not only in the United States but throughout the world. These were years in which the nations of the world, stung by participation in World War I, adopted a let's-mind-our-own-business attitude toward regulation of commerce, national defense, and international cooperation—years in which an Austrian housepainter named Adolph Hitler was allowed to build up a fanatical following. There were no changes in the American Constitution in these 12 years, but the 20th and 21st Amendments were passed in 1933, followed by 28 years in which only one Constitutional change (the 22nd, in 1951) was effected. Then came another cluster of four amendments within the ten year span, 1961–71.

How an amendment is proposed

Article Five establishes two methods of proposing amendments:

1. By a two thirds vote of a quorum of both Houses of Congress.

   or

2. By a national convention assembled by Congress after the application for a convention by two thirds (34) of the states.

All of the first 26 amendments have been proposed by the first method. Method two has been attempted several times, but never successfully. In the 1960s the late Senator Everett Dirksen (Rep., Ill.), irritated by the Supreme Court's one man, one vote decision in *Baker* v *Carr,* proposed an amendment which would have given the states control over the apportionment of state legislative districts. Dirksen chose the national convention approach and almost put it

Answer frame 12⁴

1. False. Congress may only *propose* amendments whenever two thirds of both Houses deem it necessary, but *ratification* by the legislature (or by convention) of three fourths of the states is necessary for the amendment to become effective. Amendment may also be proposed by application of the legislatures of two thirds of the states.
2. True. This is the one provision of the Constitution which is not subject to amendment without the consent of the state which would be involved.
3. True. The Constitution, laws, and treaties of the United States are to be supreme. Judges in every state are bound by this regardless of the laws of their state.
4. False. They must take an oath or affirmation *to support the Constitution,* but no religious test shall ever be required as a qualification to any office or public trust under the United States.

If you missed any of the above, reread Frame 12⁴ before beginning Chapter 5 on page 48.

Frame 1⁵ continued

over for the first time in history. By 1969, 33 legislatures (one short of the required two thirds) had petitioned Congress for a convention to act on the "Dirksen Amendment." At this critical moment, one state changed its vote and the momentum was permanently arrested.

A bill to amend the Constitution is handled by Congress in the same manner as any other measure. It is referred to the proper committee, goes through the various readings and printings, and any differences in the versions passed by House and Senate are worked out in joint conference. The only procedural differences are these:

1. An amendment must be passed by a two thirds vote rather than be a simple majority.
2. The usual bill, after passage by Congress, is sent to the president for his signature (or veto). An amendment is sent on to the states and becomes law upon ratification by three fourths of the states. Our present 50 state union requires approval by 38 states.

Curiously, the president is totally left out of a constitutional role in the amending process. He may lend the prestige of his office or exert power upon Congress as titular head of his party. As a courtesy, Congress often refers amendments to the White House for signature, but the presidential autograph is constitutionally meaningless.

How an amendment is ratified

Two methods also are provided for ratification of amendments:

1. By approval of three fourths of the state legislatures.

   or

2. By approval of conventions in three fourths of the states.

Twenty-five of the first 26 amendments have been ratified by the state legislatures.

Method two has been successfully employed only in the case of the 21st Amendment. In slightly less than 10 months (a record at that time) conventions in the required 36 states (there were only 48 at the time) approved the constitutional change which turned on the nation's liquor supply and washed out the speakeasies. The 21st is unique, too, in that it is the only amendment which drowned out a previous amendment—the 18th.

In the proposed 27th ERA (Equal Rights Amendment) two states, Tennessee and Nebraska, voted in favor of the amendment and later rescinded their approval. An interesting Constitutional problem has been thus posed: Can a state ratify an amendment and then renege? The Constitution itself is silent on this matter, and the Supreme Court to date has refused to become involved, contending that the amending process is purely political.

This, in effect, makes Congress the final arbiter. Congress has often established that a state may turn down an amendment and later vote to approve. However, it would appear that a reversal of this procedure is not valid. For example, Ohio and New Jersey ratified the 14th Amendment but later passed resolutions withdrawing their approval. Congress ignored both resolutions and the amendment, which needed approval of both states to pass, was declared ratified. All this, of course, is pure theory. There is nothing except logic which would forbid Congress from considering future changes of heart on an individual basis.

Indicate whether each of the following statements is true or false by writing "T" or "F" in the space provided.

_____ 1. The amending procedure in the Constitution was as rigid as that in the Articles of Confederation so as to avoid undercutting the intent of the Founding Fathers.

_____ 2. Other than the Bill of Rights, the Constitution has been amended only 16 times in 185 years.

_____ 3. There are two methods of proposing amendments.

_____ 4. The process for approving an amendment is identical to that of any other bill.

_____ 5. The Supreme Court must decide whether states can renege on an earlier decision to ratify an amendment.

Now turn to Answer frame 1⁵ on page 52 and check your responses.

Frame 2⁵

Briefly, let us now examine the changes made in the American Constitution.

Ten at a time

Adoption of the first ten amendments was virtually mandated by the action of those states which attached strong resolutions for a Bill of Rights to their ratification statements. The ten amendments were proposed by Congress in 1789 and ratified two years later. The basic ("inalienable" or "natural") human rights guaranteed by these amendments were in some instances practically copied from the English Declaration of Rights of 1689—which in turn mirrored pressures exerted during the mid-17th century English Puritan Revolution—and by such 17th century patriots as the great jurist, Sir Edward Coke, John Hampden (who refused to pay Charles I's levy of "ship money"), John Bate (who rusted in jail rather than pay an arbitrary duty on currants), John Pym, and John Milton (whose *Aeropagetica* is still the classic expression of the rights of freedom of speech and of the press), and many others.

The bewildering eleventh

To the nonlawyer, no other amendment is quite as mind-boggling as the 11th, which prohibits an individual from suing a state in federal court.

When Chisholm successfully sued Georgia in 1793 in the Supreme Court, the rumblings were felt in every state house in the land.

"We told you so," screamed the Antifederalists.

"They've sold us down the river," moaned the advocates of state sovereignty.

When the Constitution was up for ratification in 1787 Federalists assured voters that state sovereignty would be jealously guarded. Although Article Three, Section 2 provided that "the judicial power of the United States shall extend to controversies between an individual and a state," Federalists solemnly promised that

Answer frame 1[5]

1. False. It was not as rigid. If the procedure had been too rigid, the Constitution could not have been perfected over the years in accordance wtih changing times and conditions. This was a problem with the Articles of Confederation. Of course, if the amending procedure is too easy, the intent of the Founding Fathers could be undermined.
2. True. The first ten amendments constitute the Bill of Rights and were adopted in 1791. Since that time only 16 other amendments have been adopted. The 27th Amendment is still pending.
3. True. Amendments may be proposed by a two thirds vote of a quorum of both Houses of Congress or by a national convention assembled by Congress after the application for a convention by two thirds of the states. All of the first 26 amendments have been proposed by the first method. The second method has been unsuccessfully attempted several times.
4. False. It must be passed by a two thirds vote rather than a simple majority, and it is sent to the states and becomes law upon ratification by three fourths of the states (either by approval of three foutrhs of the state legislatures or by approval of conventions in three fourths of the states). Other bills are sent to the president for his signature (or veto). The president is left out of a constitutional role in the amending process.
5. False. The Constitution is silent on this matter, and the Supreme Court has refused to become involved. Apparently, Congress must be the final arbiter.

If you missed any of the above, reread Frame 1[5] before beginning Frame 2[5] on page 51.

Frame 2[5] continued

this provision would not apply to suits against the state except in instances where the state would give its consent.

With *Chisholm* v *Georgia* darkest fears became shining reality. Many saw the states as 13 ducks blithely swimming on a federal pond that was surrounded by armed men lying in the blinds. And a 365 day hunting season was about to open!

It had all come about when Chisholm, a resident of South Carolina serving as executor for an English creditor, brought suit against Georgia for nonpayment of a bill. The Georgia state court refused to hear the case, claiming the state could not be sued. When no other court would accept jurisdiction, the U.S. Supreme Court elected to do so. Georgia lost the suit and the high court poured salt in the wounds by pontificating at length on the subject of state sovereignty. The assurances of the Federalists had become a litany of broken promises.

So instantaneous were the yelps that the wheels of the amending process began rolling the very next day in Congress. In less than a year Congress approved an amendment protecting the states against suits by citizens of another state, or by citizens of another country. The 11th Amendment was declared ratified by the states in 1798.

The 11th Amendment was emasculated by a devastating decision in 1908. In *ex parte Young* the high court ruled that the attorney general of Minnesota, in seeking to enforce a state act which is in violation of the federal Constitution is "stripped of his official or representative character and is subjected in his person to the consequences of his individual conduct."

Nevertheless, scarcely a day passes but what some state is being sued by somebody. The magic phrase, *but not without its consent,* is still somewhat of a controlling factor.

The 11th Amendment may soon become little more than a paragraph to bewilder students who take Constitutional exams. Increasingly, the rights of the injured citizen appear to be winning out in the courts over the constitutional immunity granted the states. A body of law pinning accountability on the state for its roads, its parks, its land, and the actions of its employees seems to be pyramiding as the courts adjust to the social philosophy of the 1970s. The question of state responsibility has almost turned full circle from *Chisholm.*

The 12th Amendment—barring the Burrs

The embarrassing case of the election of 1800 showcases the necessity of an amending article which can rectify ambiguities or mistakes which the Founding Fathers failed to foresee.

Article Two, in detailing the method of election of the president and vice president, provided that the election be decided in the House whenever candidates for the two offices received the same number of votes. But when the Constitution was enacted the chance of a tie vote was considered to be remote. The Founders had failed to anticipate the rapid growth of powerful political parties. A hint of what was to develop cropped up in the election of 1796 when John Adams and C. C. Pinckney ran on the Federalist ticket against a Republican team of Thomas Jefferson and Aaron Burr. When the House met to cast ballots, Adams had the greatest number of votes. But party discipline and the rules of election were not sufficiently strong to give Pinckney the same number of votes as his running mate. As a result, Republican Adams was named president and his long-time adversary, Federalist Jefferson, became vice president. (Imagine a winning ticket of John Kennedy and Richard Nixon! Of Richard Nixon and Hubert Humphrey! Of Ted Kennedy and George Wallace!) Federalists and Republicans were both unhappy, but proposals for a correcting amendment were ignored until after the election of 1800, when a constitutional catastrophe was narrowly averted.

In 1800 the Republican candidate for president, Thomas Jefferson, and his vice presidential running mate, Aaron Burr, each received 73 electoral college votes. (John Adams received 65, C. C. Pinckney, Adams' running mate, received

64, and John Jay received one.) The people clearly believed they had elected Jefferson president and Burr vice president.

But Section 1 of Article Two provided that "The Person having the greatest Number of Votes shall be the President, if such Number be a majority of the whole Number of Electors appointed; and if there be more than one who have such Majority, and have an equal Number of Votes, then the House of Representatives shall immediately chuse by Ballot one of them for President;" The unscrupulous Burr conspired to take advantage of this constitutional ambiguity. Brazenly, he maneuvered to thwart the will of the voters and the intent of the Constitution by attempting to convince the House to name himself president and Jefferson vice president. Only the intervention of Jefferson's political antagonist, Alexander Hamilton, who threw Federalist support to Jefferson on the 36th ballot, saved the country from the rule of President Burr.

The 12th Amendment, proposed in 1803 and ratified in 1804, provided that electors "shall name in their ballots the person voted for as President, and in distinct ballots the person voted for as vice president." The electoral tragedy which almost occurred in 1800 would never happen again.

The "Civil War Amendments"

From 1861 to 1865 America drained its resources and manpower on a bitter and divisive War of the States. Upon its completion it was natural that the Constitution be adjusted to repair the inequities over which the war had been waged.

Within a period of five years, three "Civil War Amendments" were adopted. The 13th (1865) abolished slavery, the 14th (1868) conferred citizenship upon all persons born or naturalized in the United States, and the 15th (1870) secured Negro male suffrage.

Is each of the following statements true or false?

_____ 1. The Bill of Rights contained new and different human rights which had never before been codified anywhere.

_____ 2. The 11th Amendment, which prohibits an individual from suing a state in federal court, is now losing some of its significance.

_____ 3. Aaron Burr's actions were the cause of the 12th Amendment.

_____ 4. The 13th, 14th, and 15th Amendments were the result of World War II.

Now turn to Answer frame 2[5] on page 56 and check your responses.

Frame 3[5]

The most unpopular amendment

Unquestionably, the amendment which has most profoundly affected George and Suzanne Citizen is the 16th, which legalized the income tax. Adopted in 1913, it came as a follow-up of a Supreme Court decision of 1895, *Pollack* v *Farmer's Trust Co.*, which ruled that a federal income tax violated the direct tax principles of two specific clauses of Article One.

Like many monsters, the income tax came into the world as a harmless babe. The first income tax law, passed in 1913, affected only one of every 271 citizens. A married man living with his wife received a personal exemption of $4,000, a kingly sum in 1913, and then paid only 1 percent on *net* income up to $50,000. The highest surtax was 6 percent exacted on net income in excess of $500,000. Corporate net income taxes were set at 1 percent.

Direct election of senators

The 17th Amendment, also ratified in 1913, provided for direct election of U.S. senators by the people. Previously, senators had been chosen by their state legislatures. The 17th also provided for temporary filling of Senate vacancies by the governor.

The "noble experiment" to amend social habits

The only attempt to employ the amending process in an effort to regulate people's social habits came about in 1919 with ratification of the 18th Amendment. Prohibition proved to be a political Edsel. It ushered in the era of gangsters, speakeasies, moonshine, and unprecedented violence. Tens of thousands of people who disliked the taste of liquor began to drink, primarily because it was forbidden. From a purely economic standpoint, the cost of enforcement and the loss of tax revenue was staggering. After 14 frustrating years the 18th Amendment was repealed by the 21st Amendment in 1933.

The suffragettes

The idea of women participating in government by voting was never seriously contemplated by the Founding Fathers. For 131 years, federal elections were completely controlled by adult males. The 19th Amendment, ratified in 1920, brought the suffrage into the kitchen. For a couple of decades after that, husbands, fathers, and brothers did a reasonably good job of swinging the feminine vote in their families. But when Rosie the Riveter took off her apron and went into the defense industries in World War II she began to do her own political thinking. Rosie's daughters, active in today's women's lib movement, are presently engaged in extending feminine leverage in every branch of government, industry, and society.

Curiously enough, while the Constitution specifically denied suffrage to women it did not prohibit them from holding office. Thus, a woman might have run for federal office prior to 1920, but could not have voted for herself.

Although the 19th Amendment was officially proposed and ratified "after the boys came home," it is worth commenting that a great deal of the most effective politicking for the principle of the feminine vote occurred at a time when 4.8 million men were away from home and serving in the armed forces.

Clipping the "lame duck's" wings

The record showed that federal officials defeated in November elections did not always show the same sense of responsibility and dedication to duty as they had when they knew their record would be subject to the scrutiny of the voters. Consequently, some highly questionable politicking occasionally took place between the time a man was defeated in early November and the time he left office on March 4.

It took the American political system—and the amending process—144 years to plug this constitutional loophole. The 20th Amendment clipped the "lame duck's" wings. It established January 3 as the date for the opening of the new Congress and moved the presidential inauguration up from March 4 to January 20.

The modern Congress is burdened with so many details that it is practically in session the year around. Thus the defeated congressman, in spite of the framers of the 20th Amendment, still has a short period in which to vote for legislation. The election recess and the Christmas recess further reduce even that period.

Repeal of the 18th

The 21st Amendment recognized the hopelessness of the 18th.

Five amendments dealing with the electoral process

In April 1945, Franklin Roosevelt died. He had just begun his fourth term as president. No other man in history had ever been elected president more than twice. The two term precedent established by George Washington had been considered almost inviolable until 1940 when the American people chose not to "change horses in the middle of a stream"—that stream being World War II, which had opened in Europe on September 1, 1939. The 22nd Amendment, ratified in 1951, guarded against any other man serving more than two full terms as president of the United States.

The 23rd Amendment gave citizens of the District of Columbia the right to vote for president, a right historically denied them. The 23rd also assured the District of Columbia of at least the same number of electoral votes as the least populous state. No state, of course, can have fewer than three electoral votes, since it must have at least one representative and two senators.

The 24th Amendment made certain that no citizen of the United States would ever be prohibited from voting in a federal primary or election because he failed to pay a poll tax. It was adopted in 1964, at which time there were still four poll tax states in the South.

The 25th Amendment, ratified in 1967, dealt with the succession in event of death, removal from office, incapacity, or resignation of the president or vice president. Within seven years it would be applied three times.

Student protesters in the riotous 1960s and early 70s were most insistent in demanding the right of 18-year-olds to vote, claiming: "If we are old enough to be drafted and old enough to fight and die for our country, we ought to be old enough to vote." Apparently, even those who disagreed with them on other issues saw the wisdom of this demand. The 26th Amendment was approved by Congress in March 1971 and declared ratified by the states by late June. No other amendment was ever approved so swiftly!

Answer frame 2⁵

1. False. They were very similar to those contained in the English Declaration of Rights of 1689.
2. True. It may soon become insignificant in that injured citizens appear to be winning out in the courts over the immunity granted the states in the 11th Amendment. Scarcely a day goes by without some state (with its consent) being sued by somebody.
3. True. Burr tried to gain the presidency when the election was thrown into the House of Representatives even though he had run for the office of vice president. The 12th Amendment prevented the possibility of this maneuver in the future.
4. False. They were the result of the Civil War. The 13th abolished slavery, the 14th gave citizenship to all persons born or naturalized in the United States, and the 15th gave black males the right to vote.

If you missed any of the above, reread Frame 2⁵ before beginning Frame 3⁵ on page 54.

Frame 3⁵ continued

True or false?

———— 1. The 16th Amendment created a large federal income tax burden on most citizens and all corporations as soon as it was passed.

———— 2. The 17th Amendment provided for direct election of the president by the people.

———— 3. The 18th and 21st Amendments were closely related.

———— 4. The 19th Amendment created women suffrage, while the 20th Amendment ended the "lame duck" problem.

———— 5. The last five amendments all dealt with the electoral process.

Now turn to Answer frame 3⁵ on page 58 and check your responses.

Frame 4⁵

AMENDMENTS TO THE CONSTITUTION OF THE UNITED STATES*

The first ten Amendments were proposed on September 25, 1789 and were ratified on December 15, 1791. They are known as the Bill of Rights.

AMENDMENT ONE

Freedom of religion, of speech, of the press, and right of petition—Congress shall make no law respecting an establishment of religion, or prohibiting the free exercise thereof; or abridging the freedom of speech, or of the press; or the right of the people peaceably to assemble, and to petition the Government for a redress of grievances.

AMENDMENT TWO

Right of people to bear arms not to be infringed—A well-regulated militia, being necessary to the security of a free State, the right of the people to keep and bear arms, shall not be infringed.

AMENDMENT THREE

Quartering of troops—No soldier shall, in time of peace be quartered in any house, with-

* Subject headings, which do not appear in the original documents, are modifications of those to be found in *State of New Hampshire Manual for the General Court* (Concord, N.H., 1969), pp. 15–42. Spelling, punctuation, and capitalization have been modernized.

out the consent of the owner, nor in time of war, but in a manner to be prescribed by law.

AMENDMENT FOUR

Searches and seizures—The right of the people to be secure in their persons, houses, papers, and effects against unreasonable searches and seizures, shall not be violated, and no warrants shall issue, but upon probable cause, supported by oath or affirmation, and particularly describing the place to be searched, and the persons or things to be seized.

Indicate whether each of the following statements is true or false by writing "T" or "F" in the space provided.

_____ 1. The First Amendment guarantees certain basic freedoms of expression.

_____ 2. United States citizens have the right to keep and bear weapons.

_____ 3. Soldiers are free to occupy your house without your consent during a riot or other domestic crisis.

_____ 4. A search warrant is necessary before anyone can search you or your property.

Now turn to Answer frame 4[5] on page 58 and check your responses.

Frame 5[5]

AMENDMENT FIVE

Trials for crimes; just compensation for private property taken for public use—No person shall be held to answer for a capital, or otherwise infamous crime, unless on a presentment or indictment of a Grand Jury, except in cases arising in the land or naval forces, or in the militia, when in actual service in time of war or public danger; nor shall any person be subject for the same offense to be twice put in jeopardy of life or limb; nor shall be compelled in any criminal case to be a witness against himself, nor be deprived of life, liberty, or property, without due process of law; nor shall private property be taken for public use, without just compensation.

AMENDMENT SIX

Civil rights in trials for crime—In all criminal prosecutions, the accused shall enjoy the right to a speedy and public trial, by an impartial jury of the State and district wherein the crime shall have been committed, which district shall have been previously ascertained by law, and to be informed of the nature and cause of the accusation; to be confronted with the witnesses against him; to have compulsory process for obtaining witnesses in his favor, and to have the assistance of counsel for his defence.

AMENDMENT SEVEN

Civil rights in civil suits—In suits at common law, where the value in controversy shall exceed twenty dollars, the right of trial by jury shall be preserved, and no fact tried in a jury, shall be otherwise reexamined in any court of the United States, than according to the rules of the common law.

AMENDMENT EIGHT

Excessive bail, fines and punishments prohibited—Excessive bail shall not be required, nor excessive fines imposed, nor cruel and unusual punishments inflicted.

Answer frame 3⁵ ─────────────────────────────────

1. False. The first income tax law only affected one out of every 271 citizens. Corporate and individual rates were also extremely low by today's standards.
2. False. It provided for direct election of U.S. senators by the people. Formerly, they had been chosen by their state legislatures.
3. True. The 18th Amendment created prohibition, and the 21st Amendment repealed the 18th Amendment.
4. True. The 19th Amendment (in 1920) gave women the right to vote. The 20th Amendment established January 3 as the date for the opening of the new Congress and moved the presidential inauguration up from March 4 to January 20.
5. True. They guarded against any man serving more than two full terms as president (22nd), gave citizens of the District of Columbia the right to vote (23rd), outlawed the poll tax in federal primaries or elections (24th), changed the rules of succession to the office of president and vice president (25th), and gave 18 year olds the right to vote (26th).

If you missed any of the above, reread Frame 3⁵ before beginning Frame 4⁵ on page 56.

Answer frame 4⁵ ─────────────────────────────────

1. True. It guarantees freedom of religion, speech, and the press; the right to peacefully assemble; and the right to petition the government for redress of grievances.
2. True. This is guaranteed by the Second Amendment. There are, of course, certain restrictions regarding the type of weapons and where they may be carried (for example you can not walk down the street with a submachine gun).
3. False. During peacetime no soldier may be quartered in your house without your consent. In wartime a soldier may be quartered in your house only as the law permits.
4. True. A properly authorized search warrant is necessary. Otherwise the authorities could barge into your home or search you anytime they felt like it for no good reason. Upon probable cause, however, arrest and search may be made without a warrant.

If you missed any of the above, reread Frame 4⁵ before beginning Frame 5⁵ on page 57.

Frame 5⁵ continued

Indicate whether each of the following statements is true or false.

_____1. At least one of the following actions is constitutional: a civilian standing trial for murder without first being indicted by a grand jury; a witness testifying against himself; standing trial twice for the same crime; a citizen being sentenced to jail without a trial; and your home and property being taken at one tenth its fair market value to make room for a highway.

_____2. In criminal prosecutions, the accused has certain rights which are guaranteed by the Constitution.

_____3. In a civil suit involving a disputed debt of $10 a party may successfully insist on a trial by jury.

_____4. If you are arrested on a speeding charge which did not result in damage to life or property, the judge could lawfully fine you $100,000.

Now turn to answer frame 5⁵ on page 60 and check your responses.

Frame 6⁵

AMENDMENT NINE

Reserved rights of people—The enumeration in the Constitution, of certain rights, shall not be construed to deny or disparage others retained by the people.

AMENDMENT TEN

Powers not delegated, reserved to States and people—The powers not delegated to the United States by the Constitution, nor prohibited by it to the States, are reserved to the States respectively, or to the people.

AMENDMENT ELEVEN
Proposed March 4, 1794. Ratified February 7, 1795.

Judicial power of United States not to extend to suits against a State—The judicial power of the United States shall not be construed to extend to any suit in law or equity, commenced or prosecuted against one of the United States by citizens of another State, or by citizens or subjects of any foreign state.

AMENDMENT TWELVE
Proposed December 9, 1803. Ratified June 15, 1804.

Mode of electing President and Vice President*—The electors shall meet in their respective States and vote by ballot for President and Vice President, one of whom, at least, shall not be an inhabitant of the same state with themselves; they shall name in their ballots the person voted for as President, and in distinct ballots the person voted for as Vice President, and they shall make distinct lists of all persons voted for as President, and of all persons voted for as Vice President, and of the number of votes for each, which lists they shall sign and certify, and transmit sealed to the seat of the Government of the United States, directed to the President of the Senate; The President of the Senate shall, in the presence of the Senate and House of Representatives, open all the certificates and the votes shall then be counted; the person having the greatest number of votes for President, shall

be the President, if such number be a majority of the whole number of electors appointed; and if no person have such majority, then from the persons having the highest numbers not exceeding three on the list of those voted for as President, the House of Representatives shall choose immediately, by ballot, the President. But in choosing the President, the votes shall be taken by States, the representation from each State having one vote; a quorum for this purpose shall consist of a member or members from two thirds of the states, and a majority of all the states shall be necessary to a choice. And if the House of Representatives shall not choose a President whenever the right of choice shall devolve upon them, before the fourth day of March next following, then the Vice President shall act as President, as in the case of the death or other constitutional disability of the President. The Person having the greatest number of votes as Vice President, shall be the Vice President, if such number be a majority of the whole number of electors appointed, and if no person have a majority, then from the two highest numbers on the list, the Senate shall choose the Vice President; a quorum for the purpose shall consist of two thirds of the whole number of Senators and a majority of the whole number shall be necessary to a choice. But no person constitutionally ineligible to the office of President shall be eligible to that of Vice President of the United States.

---

* This has been amended by the 20th and 25th Amendments.

AMENDMENT THIRTEEN
Proposed January 31, 1865. Ratified December 6, 1865.

SECTION 1
Slavery prohibited—Neither slavery nor involuntary servitude, except as a punishment for crime whereof the party shall have been duly convicted, shall exist within the United States, or any place subject to their jurisdiction.

SECTION 2
Congress given power to enforce this article—Congress shall have power to enforce this article by appropriate legislation.

Answer frame 5⁵

1. False. All of the actions are unconstitutional under the Fifth Amendment to the Constitution.
2. True. He has the right to a speedy and public trial by an impartial jury, must be informed of the charges brought against him, is confronted by the witnesses against him, can have witnesses favorable to his side ordered to appear, and has the right to have a lawyer defend him (even if he cannot afford to pay the fee).
3. False. In civil suits the value in controversy must be in excess of $20 before the right of trial by jury is preserved.
4. False. The Eighth Amendment to the Constitution prohibits excessive bail, excessive fines, and cruel and unusual punishments.

If you missed any of the above, reread Frame 5⁵ before beginning Frame 6⁵ on page 59.

Frame 6⁵ continued

True or false?

_____ 1. Any powers which are not specifically granted to the states are to be assumed by the federal government.

_____ 2. If a citizen from Pennsylvania wants to bring suit against the state of New York he can have the case tried in a United States court.

_____ 3. In case no candidate for the presidency receives a majority of the electors' votes, the president is elected by the House; and if no candidate for vice president receives a majority, the vice president is elected by the Senate.

_____ 4. The 13th Amendment was one of great consequence.

Now turn to Answer frame 6⁵ on page 62 and check your responses.

Frame 7⁵

AMENDMENT FOURTEEN*
Proposed June 13, 1866. Ratified July 9, 1868.

SECTION 1

Citizenship defined; privileges of citizens— All persons born or naturalized in the United States, and subject to the jurisdiction thereof, are citizens of the United States, and subject to the jurisdiction thereof, are citizens of the United States and of the State wherein they reside. No State shall make or enforce any law which shall abridge the privileges or immunities of citizens of the United States; nor shall any State deprive any person of life, liberty, or property, without due process of law; nor deny to any person within its jurisdiction the equal protection of the laws.

SECTION 2

Apportionment of Representatives— Representatives shall be apportioned among the several States according to their respective numbers, counting the whole number of persons in each State, excluding Indians not taxed. But when the right to vote at any election for the choice of electors for President and Vice President of the United States, Representatives in Congress, the executive and judicial officers of a State, or the members of the Legislature thereof, is denied to any of the male inhabitants of such State, being twenty-one years of age, and citizens of the United States, or in any way abridged, except for participation in rebellion, or other crime, the basis of representation therein shall be reduced in the proportion which the number of such male citizens shall bear to the whole number of male citizens twenty-one years of age in such State.

SECTION 3

Disqualification for office; removal of disability—No person shall be a Senator or Representative in Congress, or elector of President and Vice President, or hold any office, civil or military, under the United States, or under any State, who, having previously taken an oath, as a member of Congress, or as an officer of the United States, or as a member of any State Legislature, or as an executive or judicial officer of any State, to support the Constitution of the United States, shall have engaged in insurrection or rebellion against the same, or given aid or comfort to the enemies thereof. But Congress may by a vote of two thirds of each House, remove such disability.

SECTION 4

Public debt not to be questioned; payment of debts and claims incurred in aid of rebellion

forbidden—The validity of the public debt of the United States authorized by law, including debts incurred for payment of pensions and bounties for services in suppressing insurrection or rebellion, shall not be questioned. But neither the United States nor any State shall assume or pay any debt or obligation incurred in aid of insurrection or rebellion against the United States, or any claim for the loss or emancipation of any slave; but all such debts, obligations and claims shall be held illegal and void.

SECTION 5

Congress given power to enforce this article—The Congress shall have power to enforce, by appropriate legislation, the provisions of this article.

---

* This Amendment has been the basis of several far-reaching discrimination decisions of the Supreme Court, including *Brown* v *Board of Education.*

Indicate whether each of the following statements is true or false.

_____ 1. A state may not pass a law which gives one group of citizens preferential treatment as compared with other citizens.

_____ 2. If a state should deprive the right to vote to any of its male inhabitants over 21 years of age who are citizens of the United States, it would be apportioned fewer Representatives in the House.

_____ 3. Once a person has been found guilty of insurrection or rebellion against the United States, he may never hold a state or federal office again.

_____ 4. After the Civil War, Union soldiers could be paid pensions and bounties, but Confederate soldiers could not be paid these benefits.

Now turn to Answer frame 7[5] on page 62 and check your responses.

Frame 8[5]

AMENDMENT FIFTEEN
Proposed February 28, 1869. Ratified February 3, 1870.

SECTION 1

Right of certain citizens to vote established—The right of citizens of the United States to

vote shall not be denied or abridged by the United States or by any State, on account of race, color, or previous condition of servitude.

SECTION 2

Congress given power to enforce this article—The Congress shall have power to enforce this article by appropriate legislation.

Answer frame 6⁵

1. False. It is just the other way around. Any powers not delegated to the federal government by the Constitution, nor prohibited by it to the states, are reserved for the states or to the people.
2. False. The 11th Amendment ruled out the use of the judicial power of the United States in cases where a state is sued by citizens of another state or of a foreign country.
3. True. The 12th Amendment established this procedure. (Although there has been talk of having direct election by the people, the "electoral college" is still in effect.) In elections of the president in the House each state would have only one vote.
4. True. It was of major consequence since it prohibited slavery.

If you missed any of the above, reread Frame 6⁵ before beginning Frame 7⁵ on page 60.

Answer frame 7⁵

1. True. A state may not deny to any person within its jurisdiction the equal protection of the laws. This means that everyone should have equally fair treatment under the law.
2. True. The 14th Amendment provided this. Its purpose was to encourage all states to allow all male citizens (this was before women's suffrage) who met these qualifications (including blacks in the southern states) to vote.
3. False. Congress, by a vote of two thirds of each House, can remove this disability and permit the person to again hold office.
4. True. The United States could pay (without question) pensions and bounties for services in suppressing insurrection or rebellion, but neither the United States nor any state could pay any debt incurred in aid of insurrection or rebellion against the United States. This meant the southern states had to help pay the costs of the war but could not pay back creditors from whom they had borrowed to fight the war.

If you missed any of the above, reread Frame 7⁵ before beginning Frame 8⁵ on page 61.

Frame 8⁵ continued

AMENDMENT SIXTEEN
Proposed July 2, 1909. Ratified February 3, 1913.

Taxes on incomes—The Congress shall have power to lay and collect taxes on incomes, from whatever sources derived, without apportionment among the several States, and without regard to any census or enumeration.

AMENDMENT SEVENTEEN
Proposed May 13, 1912. Ratified April 8, 1913.

SECTION 1

Election of United States Senators; filling of vacancies; qualification of electors—The Senate of the United States will be composed of two Senators from each State, elected by the people thereof, for six years; and each Senator shall have one vote. The electors in each State shall have the qualifications requisite for electors of the most numerous branch of the State Legislatures.

SECTION 2

When vacancies happen in the representation of any State in the Senate, the executive authority of such State shall issue writs of election to fill such vacancies: Provided, that the legislature of any State may empower the Executive thereof to make temporary appointment until the people fill the vacancies by election as the Legislature may direct.

SECTION 3

This amendment shall not be so construed as to affect the election or term of any Senator chosen before it becomes valid as part of the Constitution.

AMENDMENT EIGHTEEN°

Proposed December 18, 1917. Ratified January 16, 1919.

SECTION 1

Liquors, for beverage purposes, prohibited—After one year from the ratification of this article the manufacture, sale, or transportation of intoxicating liquors within, the importation thereof into, or the exportation thereof from the United States and all territory subject to the jurisdiction thereof for beverage purposes is hereby prohibited.

SECTION 2

Legislation to enforce this article—The Congress and the several States shall have concurrent power to enforce this article by appropriate legislation.

SECTION 3

Ratification—This article shall be inoperative unless it shall have been ratified as an amendment to the Constitution by the Legislatures of the several States, as provided in the Constitution within seven years from the date of the submission hereof to the States by the Congress.

° This amendment was repealed by the 21st Amendment, effective December 5, 1933.

Indicate whether each of the following statements is true or false.

_____ 1. The right of former slaves to vote was affirmed by the 15th Amendment.

_____ 2. The 16th Amendment specifically gave Congress the power to collect taxes from any and all sources.

_____ 3. Senators have always been elected directly by the people of their state.

_____ 4. The 18th Amendment led the nation into an era of prohibition which lasted almost 14 years.

Now turn to Answer frame 8⁵ on page 64 and check your responses.

Frame 9⁵ ─────────────────────────

AMENDMENT NINETEEN

Proposed June 4, 1919. Ratified August 18, 1920.

The right of citizens to vote shall not be denied because of sex—1. The right of citizens of the United States to vote shall not be denied or abridged by the United States or by any State on account of sex.

2. Congress shall have power to enforce this article by appropriate legislation.

AMENDMENT TWENTY

Proposed March 2, 1932. Ratified January 23, 1933.

SECTION 1

Terms of President, Vice President, Senators and Representatives—The terms of the President and Vice President shall end at noon on the 20th day of January, and the terms of Senators and Representatives at noon on the 3d day of January, of the years in which such terms

Answer frame 8⁵ ───

1. True. It said the right to vote cannot be denied because of race, color, or previous conditions of servitude.
2. True. And there was no requirement that there be a proportional amount from each state.
3. False. Until the 17th Amendment (ratified in 1913) they had been elected by their State Legislatures.
4. True. The 18th Amendment was ratified in early 1919, became effective in 1920, and was repealed in late 1933. It prohibited the manufacture, sale, or transportation of intoxicating liquors.

If you missed any of the above, reread Frame 8⁵ before beginning Frame 9⁵ on page 63.

Frame 9⁵ continued

would have ended if this article had not been ratified; and the terms of their successors shall then begin.

SECTION 2

Time of assembling Congress—The Congress shall assemble at least once in every year, and such meeting shall begin at noon on the 3d day of January, unless they shall by law appoint a different day.

SECTION 3

Filling vacancy in office of President—If, at the time fixed for the beginning of the term of the President, the President elect shall have died, the Vice President elect shall become President. If a President shall not have been chosen before the time fixed for the beginning of his term, or if the President elect shall have failed to qualify, then the Vice President elect shall act as President until a President shall have qualified; and the Congress may by law provide for the case wherein neither a President elect nor a Vice President elect shall have qualified, declaring who shall then act as President, or the manner in which one who is to act shall be selected, and such person shall act accordingly

until a President or Vice President shall have qualified.

SECTION 4

Power of Congress in Presidential succession—The Congress may by law provide for the case of the death of any of the persons from whom the House of Representatives may choose a President whenever the right of choice shall have devolved upon them, and for the case of the death of any of the persons from whom the Senate may choose a Vice President whenever the right of choice shall have devolved upon them.

SECTION 5

Time of taking effect—Sections 1 and 2 shall take effect on the 15th day of October following the ratification of this article.

SECTION 6

Ratification—This article shall be inoperative unless it shall have been ratified as an amendment to the Constitution by the Legislatures of three fourths of the several States within seven years from the date of its submission.

Indicate whether each of the following statements is true or false.

_____ 1. Women's suffrage was not granted in all states until 1920.

_____ 2. Congress normally begins its sessions on the 20th day of January.

_____ 3. If a president has not been chosen by inauguration day or if he has failed to qualify, then the vice president elect shall become president.

_____ 4. Congress in certain instances may make laws regarding the procedures for selecting a president and vice president.

Now turn to Answer frame 9⁵ on page 66 and check your responses.

Frame 10[5]

AMENDMENT TWENTY-ONE
Proposed February 20, 1933. Ratified December 5, 1933.

Section 1

Repeal of Prohibition Amendment—The eighteenth article of amendment to the Constitution of the United States is hereby repealed.

Section 2

Transportation of intoxicating Liquors—The transportation or importation into any State, Territory, or Possession of the United States for delivery or use therein of intoxicating liquors, in violation of the laws thereof, is hereby prohibited.

Section 3

Ratification—This article shall be inoperative unless it shall have been ratified as an amendment to the Constitution by conventions in the several States, as provided in the Constitution, within seven years from the date of the submission hereof to the States by the Congress.

AMENDMENT TWENTY-TWO
Proposed March 24, 1947. Ratified February 27, 1951.

Section 1

Term of the office of President—No person shall be elected to the office of the President more than twice, and no person who has held the office of President, or acted as President, for more than two years of a term to which some other person was elected President shall be elected to the office of the President more than once. But this article shall not apply to any person holding the office of President when this article was proposed by the Congress, and shall not prevent any person who may be holding the office of President, or acting as President, during the term within which this article becomes operative from holding the office of President or

acting as President during the remainder of such term.

Section 2

Ratification—This article shall be inoperative unless it shall have been ratified as an amendment to the Constitution by the legislatures of three fourths of the several States within seven years from the date of its submission to the States by the Congress.

AMENDMENT TWENTY-THREE
Proposed June 16, 1960. Ratified March 29, 1961.

Section 1

District of Columbia—The District constituting the seat of Government of the United States shall appoint in such manner as the Congress may direct:

A number of electors of President and Vice President equal to the whole number of Senators and Representatives in Congress to which the District would be entitled if it were a State, but in no event more than the least populous State; they shall be in addition to those appointed by the States, but they shall be considered, for the purposes of the election of President and Vice President, to be electors appointed by a State; and they shall meet in the District and perform such duties as provided by the twelfth article of amendment.

Section 2

Congress given power to enforce this article—The Congress shall have power to enforce this article by appropriate legislation.

AMENDMENT TWENTY-FOUR
Proposed August 27, 1962. Ratified January 23, 1964.

Section 1

Relating to the qualifications of electors—The rights of citizens of the United States to vote in any primary or other election for President or

Answer frame 9[5]

1. True. Only nine states permitted women to vote before the 19th Amendment was passed. The Amendment required it in all states.
2. False. It normally begins its sessions on the 3rd day of January. The 20th of January is inauguration day for new presidents and vice presidents.
3. False. In this circumstance the vice president elect will *act* as president until a president shall have qualified. If the president elect dies before his term is to start, then the vice president elect would become president on inauguration day.
4. True. When the House is to choose a president and one of those under consideration dies, the Congress may make laws which declare what to do about selecting a president. The same is true for the Senate in selecting a vice president.

If you missed any of the above, reread Frame 9[5] before beginning Frame 10[5] on page 65.

Frame 10[5] continued

Vice President, for electors for President or Vice President, or for Senator or Representative in Congress, shall not be denied or abridged by the United States or any State by reason of failure to pay any poll tax or other tax.

SECTION 2

Congress given power to enforce this article —The Congress shall have power to enforce this article by appropriate legislation.

Indicate whether each of the following statements is true or false.

_____ 1. The 21st Amendment prohibits any state from forbidding the manufacture, sale, or transportation of intoxicating liquors within that state.

_____ 2. Gerald Ford could be elected to the office of president in 1976 and 1980.

_____ 3. The 23rd Amendment gave the citizens of the District of Columbia the right to vote for persons running for the offices of president and vice president.

_____ 4. Until 1964, voters in some states were denied the right to vote if they did not pay a poll tax.

Now turn to Answer frame 10[5] on page 65 and check your responses.

Frame 11[5]

AMENDMENT TWENTY-FIVE
Proposed January 6, 1965. Ratified February 23, 1967.

SECTION 1

Vice President to become President—In case of the removal of tne President from office or of his death or resignation, the Vice President shall become President.

SECTION 2

President to nominate Vice President when vacancy in office of Vice President—Whenever there is a vacancy in the office of the Vice President, the President shall nominate a Vice President who shall take office upon confirmation by a majority vote of both houses of Congress.

SECTION 3

President unable to discharge duties; Vice President to be Acting President—Whenever the President transmits to the President pro tempore of the Senate and the Speaker of the House of Representatives his written declaration that he is unable to discharge the powers and duties of his office, and until he transmits to them a written declaration to the contrary, such powers and duties shall be discharged by the Vice President as Acting President.

SECTION 4

President unable to discharge duties: how determined—Whenever the Vice President and a majority of either of the principal officers of the executive departments or of such other body as Congress may by law provide, transmit to the President pro tempore of the Senate and the Speaker of the House of Representatives their written declaration that the President is unable to discharge the powers and duties of his office, the Vice President shall immediately assume the powers and duties of the office as Acting President.

Thereafter, when the President transmits to the President pro tempore of the Senate and the Speaker of the House of Representatives his written declaration that no inability exists, he shall resume the powers and duties of his office unless the Vice President and a majority of either the principal officers of the executive department or of such other body as Congress may by law provide, transmit within four days to the President pro tempore of the Senate and the Speaker of the House of Representatives their written declaration that the President is unable to discharge the powers and duties of his office. Thereupon Congress shall decide the issue, assembling within forty-eight hours for that purpose if not in session. If the Congress, within twenty-one days after receipt of the latter written declaration, or, if Congress is not in session,

within twenty-one days after Congress is required to assemble, determines by two thirds vote of both Houses that the President is unable to discharge the powers and duties of his office, the Vice President shall continue to discharge the same as Acting President; otherwise, the President shall resume the powers and duties of his office.

AMENDMENT TWENTY-SIX
Proposed March 23, 1971. Ratified July 1, 1971.

SECTION 1

The right of citizens eighteen years of age or older to vote—The right of citizens of the United States, who are eighteen years of age or older, to vote shall not be denied or abridged by the United States or by any State on account of age.

SECTION 2

Congress given power to enforce this article—The Congress shall have power to enforce this article by appropriate legislation.

AMENDMENT TWENTY-SEVEN
Proposed March 22, 1972. Ratification pending.

SECTION 1

The equality of rights under law shall not be denied because of sex—Equality of rights under law shall not be denied or abridged by the United States or any State on account of sex.

SECTION 2

Congress given power to enforce this article—The Congress shall have the power to enforce by appropriate legislation the provisions of this article.

SECTION 3

Time of taking effect—This Amendment shall take effect two years after the date of ratification.

Answer frame 10[5]

1. False. It left the decision on prohibition up to each state. And if certain states decide to have prohibition, others must not violate these state laws.
2. False. He will have served more than two years of Nixon's last term. Therefore, he may not be elected to the office of president more than once.
3. True. Until this amendment passed in 1961 residents of the District of Columbia did not have this right.
4. True. This was a method used by some southern states to keep blacks from voting (it also prevented poor whites from voting). The 24th Amendment prohibited this practice.

If you missed any of the above, reread Frame 10[5] before beginning Frame 11[5] on page 66.

Frame 11[5] continued

Is each of the following statements true or false?

_____ 1. When Spiro Agnew vacated the office of vice president, the Senate elected his successor, Gerald Ford.

_____ 2. When the president declares in writing that he is unable to discharge the powers and duties of his office the vice president becomes the president.

_____ 3. The vice president and certain others may decide on their own that the president is unable to discharge the powers and duties of his office, in which event the vice president becomes acting president.

_____ 4. The 26th Amendment reduced the voting age from 21 to 18.

_____ 5. The 27th Amendment was ratified in 1973 and gave equal rights to women.

Now turn to Answer frame 11[5] on page 70 and check your responses.

chapter 6

THE JUDICIARY

Frame 1[6]

Most of the Founding Fathers had legal backgrounds. Since lawyers are notorious for their verbal stamina and since our present federal judicial system, to most lay people, seems a bewildering network of appellate, district, and special courts, it would seem natural that the Judicial Article would be lengthy and labyrinthian, loaded with "whereases," "pursuants," and such legalisms as "affirming a petition to deny."

On the contrary, Article Three is as short and simple as a bachelor's grocery list. Its essence is contained in the first 30 words:

The judicial power of the United States shall be vested in one Supreme Court, and in such inferior courts as the Congress may from time to time ordain and establish.

All the rest is academic. Federal judges, if they behave (says Section 1) may serve for life at salaries which cannot be reduced. Section 2 broadly determines which cases fall within the federal judicial power. The previous Article (Article Two, dealing with the executive authority) vested the president with the power to name all federal judges, subject to advice and consent of the Senate.

How many Supreme Court judges shall there be? How much shall they be paid? What kind of "inferior" courts should be established? What qualifications must a judge have? Should they wear pink or white or green or black robes?

On these and dozens of other questions the Constitution is silent. Just as the chairman of the board leaves the annual picnic details—right down to the amount of mayonnaise in the potato salad—to the picnic committee, the Constitution delegated the judicial details to the Congress.

Acutely aware that lack of a federal judiciary was one of the major deficiencies of the Articles of Confederation, Congress responded by passing the Judiciary Act of 1789. The number of Supreme Court justices was set at six (political infighting and expansion of the frontiers caused this number to vary between five and ten until 1869 when the present nine man Court was established).

District and appellate courts were also established and have increased with population and territorial growth until today there are 86 district courts and 11 appellate divisions.

Today's intricate federal court system is based substantially upon the simple provisions of Article III of the Constitution, implemented by the Ellsworth Judiciary Act of 1789, and occasionally modified by a piece of "growing pains" legislation.

Marbury v Madison

Section 13 of the Judiciary Act of 1789 provided that under certain circumstances a petitioner might ask the Supreme Court for a writ of mandamus (requiring an official to perform a specific act or duty).

Paragraph 2, Section 2 of Article Three of the Constitution stipulated that except for certain special instances (cases affecting ambassadors, for example) the Supreme Court shall be limited to *appellate jurisdiction*. This meant that

Answer frame 11⁵

1. False. Under the 25th Amendment (ratified in 1967) the president nominates a vice president when that office becomes vacant, and the nominee must be confirmed by a majority vote of both Houses of Congress.
2. False. He becomes the *acting* president until the president is again able to discharge the powers and duties of his office.
3. True. The vice president and a majority of either of the principal officers of the executive departments (the cabinet) or of such other body as Congress may by law provide, may declare in writing to the leader of the Senate and the Speaker of the House that the president cannot perform his duties. The vice president does then become acting president. This same group can ask Congress to decide whether a president is fit to resume his duties if they do not think he is.
4. True. And one of the arguments that led to this Amendment was that if young men were old enough to fight and die for their country they were old enough to vote.
5. False. As of June 1975 it has not been ratified.

If you missed any of the above, reread Frame 11⁵ before beginning Chapter 6 on page 69.

Frame 1⁶ continued

the Court would only hear appeals from lower courts; that cases would not *originate* in the Supreme Court.

Take these two seemingly innocent and unrelated clauses. Add the bitter Antifederalist court attitude held by Thomas Jefferson and his Republicans, who came to power in 1801. Throw in a trifling, pittance paying justice of the peace job in the District of Columbia which the Republicans did not want to give the Federalists. Hand the mixture and mixer to a courageous, clear-thinking chief justice with a sense of historic timing that may never be excelled in the annals of American jurisprudence, and you have the ingredients for the most famous case in American Constitutional history.

Just before he left the presidency in 1801, John Adams appointed 42 men to justiceships of the peace in the Washington, D.C., area. The appointments were routinely confirmed by the Senate and the commissions properly signed and sealed. *But the secretary of state neglected to deliver the commissions.* Suddenly it was too late; John Adams and his Federalists were out of office and a new breed of politicians were in.

Thomas Jefferson, first president to set up housekeeping in the White House, was inaugurated in March 1801. Promptly, he ordered his

secretary of state, James Madison, to commission 25 of Adams' "midnight appointments" but to withhold the other 17 commissions. Among those denied jobs was a man named William Marbury and three genuine historical et ceteras named Dennis Ramsay, William Harper, and Robert Townsend Hooe. The four petitioned the high court for a writ of mandamus ordering Madison to deliver their commissions. The 13 others who were denied jobs did not join in the suit, possibly because they did not want the jobs, probably because the petty position did not justify the expense.

Chief Justice Marshall routinely ordered Secretary of State Madison to show cause why the writ should not be awarded. But the Jeffersonians voted to cancel the June 1802, session of the Supreme Court. *Marbury* v *Madison* simmered on the docket until 1803. By this time one half of the period of the five year terms of office for which the men had been appointed had expired.

Marbury v *Madison* can only be appreciated when viewed in proper historical perspective. The position of Supreme Court justice was a demeaning one in the early Jeffersonian period, and a substantial section of the public was openly disrespectful of the Court. Indeed, John

Jay, first chief justice of the Supreme Court, resigned in disgust in 1805 because of conditions which he believed were hopeless.

Justice Marshall considered the Marbury case with the realization that the House of Representatives had just impeached a United States justice—John Pickering of the District Court of New Hampshire. The Republican-dominated house in Pennsylvania had impeached Judge Alexander Addison. Now the Republicans in Washington were moving openly to remove Justice Chase from the Supreme Court. The word was out, at first in the congressional cloakrooms and in whispered conversations at society gatherings, and later openly: John Marshall was next if the high court ordered Madison to deliver the commissions. Furthermore, Marshall realized that the court lacked the physical means to compel execution of the commissions. In the words of Marshall's biographer, Albert Beveridge, "Jefferson would have denounced the illegality of such a decision and laughed at the court's predicament."

The alternative—to admit that Jefferson need not comply with a properly signed and executed appointment—was equally disagreeable to Marshall. It would have been a sign of weakness and might have set a precedent for executive supremacy which might some day come back to haunt the other branches.

In handling the dilemma, John Marshall satisfied neither William Marbury nor the Jeffersonians who refused to let Marbury become a justice of the peace. Instead, he chose this trifling case as a pretext for reaching the springboard from which he would leap to judicial immortality. Brave, bold, creative, surprising, shocking, ingenious—these are but a few of the terms which history has used to characterize the judicial strategy employed in *Marbury* v *Madison*.

Did William Marbury have a right to his commission as justice of the peace?

Yes, said Marshall in a few thousand words. For President Adams had signed the commission and the secretary of state had duly affixed the seal of the United States thereto.

If Mr. Marbury's rights were violated, does he have legal redress?

Of course, ruled Justice Marshall. Wherever an inequity exists under the Constitution, a proper remedy must always be available.

Has Mr. Marbury taken the proper remedy in seeking a mandamus from the Supreme Court?

It was in his totally unexpected, refreshingly original, and now world famous reply to this question that John Marshall shaped the course of American History.

William Marbury, Marshall ruled, had no right to ask the Supreme Court for a writ of mandamus. For the Supreme Court is a Court of appellate jurisdiction. Except in a few enumerated instances, the Court does not have original jurisdiction.

If Section 13 of the Judiciary Act of 1789 provides that Mr. Marbury may seek mandamus in the Supreme Court, that Section is patently opposed to the spirit of Article III of the Constitution. The Judiciary Act of 1789 is thereby unconstitutional.

The important thing for the student to remember is that the Judiciary Act of 1789 *was an act of Congress*. Standing in the shadow of impeachment at a moment when the Supreme Court commanded neither public trust nor congressional respect, John Marshall established the Court as the umpire which would forever after declare "safe" or "out" on legislative actions of the Congress.

Judicial review—this power of the courts to rule on legislation—*is a uniquely American contribution to the science of government and jurisprudence*. It remained distinctly American for 140 years. Not until after World War II, when West Germany, Italy, and Japan also tried it, did any other government of any importance set up a similar system. (The Italian and Japanese experiments have not been successful.)

It is one of the amazing ironies of political science that there is no mention of judicial review in the American Constitution. Alexander Hamilton thoroughly subscribed to the principle in *The Federalist*. As precedents, several state courts had invalidated state legislation on constitutional grounds. In 1796 the U.S. Supreme Court, assuming the power to rule on acts of Congress, found a federal statute was in harmony with the Constitution (*Hylton* v *U.S.*). But since nothing was upset, neither the decision nor the principle it established was widely noticed.

Since Article Four declared the Constitution is "the supreme law of the land" and since Article Three extends the power of the federal courts to cases arising from the Constitution, loose constructionists believed that interpretation of this "supreme law" was clearly the province of the courts. These are some of the bases from which Marshall took his authority.

Indicate whether each of the following statements is true or false by writing "T" or "F" in the space provided.

———— 1. Article Three, the Judicial Article of the Constitution, is extremely "wordy" and complex, covering every minor detail in great depth.

———— 2. The Constitution does not even state the number of Supreme Court judges there shall be.

———— 3. The Supreme Court had power, prestige, and acceptance by the other branches and the people from the time it was established.

———— 4. The real significance of the *Marbury* v *Madison* case was that it established the right of judicial review of federal legislation.

Now turn to Answer frame 1[6] on page 74 to check your responses.

Frame 2[6]

The Marshall era

Just as a good parent influences a child's entire life by the example set during the formative years, so did John Marshall of Virginia shape the Constitutional destiny of a young nation. Though his rulings generally reflected his Federalist principles favoring a strong central authority and the sanctity of property, they were always bulwarked by chapter, verse, and spirit of his living *Bible*, the Constitution.

It is no accident that historians, writing of the period from 1801–35, use the words "John Marshall" and "Supreme Court" synonymously. Marshall's grasp of issues was so keen, his research so scrupulous, his logic so devastating, his opinions so irrefutable that in five of his landmark decisions (*Marbury* v *Madison, McCulloch* v *Maryland, Fletcher* v *Peck, Cohens* v *Virginia* and *Barron* v *Baltimore*) he swept the entire court.

William Marbury, somewhat to the satisfaction of the Jeffersonians, never did get his job. History does not record that he, or the millions of law students and political science majors who have since studied "M & M," ever really cared. If any reader is looking for a bit of historical trivia to spring on an unsuspecting lawyer friend or history buff, ask for the name of the secretary of state under John Adams who carelessly neglected to deliver the commission for William Marbury.

The answer, of course, is John Marshall! Truth surely is stranger than fiction.

Though *Marbury* v *Madison* was his masterpiece, John Marshall lighted other beacons which are still illuminating constitutional runways in the 1970s.

In *McCulloch* v *Maryland* (1819) he put the federal-state relationship in permanent focus with his much quoted "the power to tax is the power to destroy" ruling which declared invalid a Maryland tax on a federally chartered bank in Baltimore. Thus was born the doctrine of implied powers.

In 1816 the Marshall court, in an opinion written by Justice Story, held unanimously (*Martin* v *Hunter's Lessee*) that the Supreme Court had the authority to overthrow judgments of *state* courts which are not in harmony with the *federal* constitution. This authority was extended to criminal proceedings of state courts in Mr. Marshall's opinion delivered in the landmark case of *Cohens* v *Virginia* in 1821.

In *Fletcher* v *Peck* (1810) the Supreme Court, affirming the sanctity of a contract even in the case of state legislation nullifying that contract, proclaimed the Court's right to overthrow state legislation which is out of step with the federal constitution.

John Marshall participated in more than 1,100 decisions of the Supreme Court, and personally wrote over 500 opinions. Forty-four of his rulings were on delicate constitutional issues, covering almost every debatable clause. He also presided with distinction at the trials of Aaron Burr and Samuel Chase.

Dred Scott v Sanford (1857)

It was 54 years after *Marbury* before the Supreme Court overturned another act of Congress.

Dred Scott was a black piece of property who was shuttled with his master's suitcase and shaving mug from slave to free to slave territory. His suit for freedom, on grounds that he had lived in the free state of Illinois, was taken out of the Missouri state courts and wound up in the federal court system, eventually coming before the Supreme Court.

In his majority opinion, Chief Justice Taney turned down Dred Scott's plea for freedom. He held that Scott was the property of his master and not a citizen under the terms of the Constitution. Since he was not a citizen he had no right to bring suit in a federal court. The vote was seven to two, but the findings were so complex that all nine judges entered separate opinions on one or more points.

But Taney was not satisfied merely to deny Dred Scott's appeal for freedom. The Court went on to overthrow the Missouri Compromise of 1820, an act of Congress which prohibited slavery north of an arbitrarily-drawn geographical line. *Dred Scott* v *Sandford* brought on the darkest day in the history of judicial review. It was a decision that took a Civil War and a 13th Amendment to undo.

FDR and judicial review

No president ever felt the sting of judicial review as deeply as Franklin D. Roosevelt.

Coming into office in March 1933, in the midst of the most devastating depression in the history of the nation, FDR proposed an ambitious program of legislation calculated to raise wages, limit production of farm products, encourage industry, and generally grease the wheels of progress. An enthusiastic Democratic Congress promptly converted the proposals into law.

In January 1935, the Supreme Court began its review of the constitutionality of the New Deal. By the middle of the following year eight cases had been decided against Roosevelt. Invalidated, in succession, were Section 9 (c) of the National Industrial Recovery Act, then the NIRA (or NRA) itself, the Railroad Pension Act, the Farm Mortgage program, the Agricultural Adjustment Act, amendments to the AAA, the Bituminous Coal Act, and the Municipal Bankruptcy Act. Only the TVA (Tennessee Valley Authority—a vast federal program to bring cheap electricity to a section of the country) and the emergency monetary measures adopted in the early days of Roosevelt's term were given qualified approval.

Their program shattered by "nine old men," Democrats quickly countered with proposals to abridge the Court's control over acts of Congress. Senator Joseph O'Mahoney of Wyoming proposed an amendment which would require a two thirds vote of the Supreme Court to overthrow an act of Congress. Senator Burton K. Wheeler of Montana submitted an amendment which would have allowed Congress to "veto the Court's veto"—override the Supreme Court's invalidation of a law by a two thirds vote of the House and Senate. Other suggestions were not so mild. A few militants openly suggested stripping the Court of its prerogative of judicial review.

In November 1936, American voters gave Roosevelt what was at the time the greatest plurality in the history of the American presidency. The Republicans carried only Maine and Vermont. Fresh from this triumph, which he interpreted as a mandate to continue his New Deal program, FDR subtly responded in 1937 with a plan to reorganize the federal judiciary. For every 70 year old judge with ten or more years of service on the federal bench, the president would be authorized to appoint an additional justice. Maximum number of appointments

Answer frame 1⁶ _____

1. False. It is extremely short and simple in its wording and left many details open for Congress to decide. Today's intricate court system is based on the simple provisions of Article Three of the Constitution as implemented by the Judiciary Act of 1789 (with a few changes by Congress since that time).
2. True. Congress (in 1789) set the number at six. Since that time it has varied between five and ten until 1869 when the present nine-man Court was established.
3. False. The position of Supreme Court justice was a demeaning one in the early Jeffersonian period. A substantial portion of the public was openly disrespectful of the Court. The first chief justice, John Jay, had resigned in disgust in 1805 because of conditions which he believed to be hopeless. One justice was under pressure of removal, and the word was out that John Marshall was next if the Court ordered Madison to deliver the commissions to Marbury and others.
4. True. John Marshall led the Court to rule that Section 13 of the Judiciary Act of 1789 was unconstitutional since it was opposed to the spirit of Article Three of the Constitution. There is no mention of judicial review in the Constitution.

If you missed any of the above, reread Frame 1⁶ before beginning Frame 2⁶ on page 72.

Frame 2⁶ continued

—50; maximum on the Supreme Court—15. Object? To lessen the work load and infuse younger blood into the system, for obviously a 70 year old employee does not have the vigor and capacity of a 50 year old.

One thing FDR had going for him: if the plan became law, the Court would have virtually no chance of overthrowing it. Article Three clearly left the composition of the federal judiciary to the discretion of the Congress.

No president ever soothed the American voter with the Pied Piper persuasiveness of Franklin D. Roosevelt. The magic of his radio voice was beamed to millions in Sunday evening "fireside chats" which spread the gospel of confidence and cheer and concern for humanity. "Every time he opens his mouth, it costs me a million votes," lamented Alfred Landon, his Republican opponent in 1936.

But not even Franklin Roosevelt could sell the "court-packing plan" to the American people. The Republican press almost unanimously interpreted it as a Machiavellian scheme to undermine the last bastion of objectivity remaining in government. Disagreement over its merits brought about the first significant split in Roosevelt's own party, the most mortal blow being the defection of Virginia Senator Carter Glass, "father" of the Federal Reserve System.

In July 1937, the U.S. Senate defeated the bill and returned it to the Judiciary Committee to die unlamented.

The court packing proposal brought unexpected Democratic dividends, however. While the measure was before the Congress and the country, a new series of New Deal legislative enactments was before the courts. In an amazing philosophical flip-flop, the Supreme Court began to accept principles it had previously opposed.

Much of the New Deal legislation had been overturned by close margins. The extreme reactionaries and flaming liberals remained unchanged, but the "moderates"—notably Justice Roberts and Chief Justice Hughes—switched to the New Deal point of view.

Many factors probably contributed to this change of heart. Hughes and Roberts had always been moderates with open minds. The legislation before the courts in 1937 had been fashioned with the Supreme Court objections of 1935 in mind. But the political implications of continued wholesale slaughter of the popular New Deal program could not have been lost on these two distinguished jurists.

The first hint of a liberal breeze blew early in 1937 when the Court approved, five to four, a state of Washington minimum wage law which was similar to a New York statute declared unconstitutional only the year before, also by a five to four vote. In both cases, the affirmative votes of four liberal judges matched the dissents of four conservatives. Mr. Roberts' switch from the conservative to the liberal viewpoint brought about the change.

Quickly, the Court proceeded to give its blessing to the Farm Mortgage Act, the National Labor Relations Act, and the Social Security Act.

At this point the grim reaper and the rock-ing chair stepped in to accomplish what the House and Senate had been unable to do: permit Franklin Roosevelt to pack the Supreme Court with men of the New Deal spirit. Arch-conservative Willis Van de Vanter resigned in May 1937, and was replaced by the liberal Hugo L. Black. In the next seven years FDR made seven additional appointments. The liberal nationalistic social philosophy was assured of clear sailing in judicial waters. Franklin Roosevelt had lost the battle and won the war.

Indicate whether each of the following statements is true or false.

_____ 1. John Marshall became "a legend in his own time."

_____ 2. The Dred Scott decision was one of the brightest spots in the history of the Court regarding judicial review of federal legislation.

_____ 3. The New Deal legislative program of Franklin D. Roosevelt was initially thwarted by the process of judicial review.

_____ 4. Roosevelt was eventually able to fill the positions on the Court with liberals.

Now turn to Answer frame 2⁶ on page 76 and check your responses.

Frame 3⁶

The Warren court

The "Warren court," so named because of the leadership provided by Chief Justice Earl Warren from 1953 to 1969, is best remembered for its landmark decisions in cases involving human values.

In *Brown* v *Board of Education of Topeka* (1954) the Court addressed itself to the question: Does public school segregation, based solely upon race, deprive children of the minority group of equal educational opportunities?

In the most reverberating decision of the 20th century, the Court unanimously held, in essence, that black children in all-black schools—even where all standards are "white"—are deprived of equal educational opportunities.

The mid-20th century movement of citizens from rural to urban areas was seldom accompanied by any adjustment in the legislative representation of the affected electoral districts. This imbalance enabled small towns and farming communities to exercise disproportionate control of many state legislatures. The Warren court struck at this inequity (*Baker* v *Carr*, 1962) with its now famous "one man, one vote" ruling which declared that federal courts properly have jurisdiction in cases involving state legislative apportionment.

Baker v *Carr*, in its long-range effect, may go down in history as one of the most far reaching decisions in American political history—a decision that will turn over governmental reins to a new ruling class.

Two other declarations of the Warren Court have had bulldozer impact on the American way of life. *Escobedo* v *Illinois* (1964) and *Miranda* v *Arizona* (1966) underlined the constitutional rights of arrested persons to be represented by counsel and to be warned that any statements they make can be used to incriminate them.

The Nixon-Burger court

Four quick vacancies on the Supreme Court, beginning in 1969, offered Richard Nixon an un-

Answer frame 2⁶

1. True. He shaped the Constitutional destiny of the young nation. He brought the Supreme Court to a position of great respect. His grasp of ideas was keen, his research scrupulous, his logic devastating, and his opinion irrefutable. His name became synonymous with "Supreme Court."

2. False. It occurred in 1857 and was the darkest day of judicial review. It overturned the Missouri Compromise of 1820, an act of Congress which prohibited slavery north of an arbitrarily-drawn geographical line. The Civil War and the 13th Amendment (abolishing slavery) followed shortly thereafter.

3. True. Most of the early legislation of the New Deal was declared unconstitutional by the Supreme Court. In response, Roosevelt tried to increase the size of the Court. But not even he could sell the "court packing plan" to the American people. Eventually the day was saved when a new series of New Deal legislative enactments came before the Court and were not found to be unconstitutional. Some of the moderates on the Court had changed their stance.

4. True. He was able to make eight appointments to the Court due to retirements and deaths. The new men were "men of the New Deal spirit."

If you missed any of the above, reread Frame 2⁶ before beginning Frame 3⁶ on page 75.

Frame 3⁶ continued

usual opportunity of shaping the Court according to his own middle-of-the-road principles. While it is still too early to make an accurate assessment, it appears after five years that Mr. Nixon did not quite achieve his goal.

In *in re Winship* (1970) the Court continued in the path established by the Warren court (*in re Gault*, 1967) in demonstrating concern for the long neglected rights of juveniles charged with crimes. The *Roe* v *Wade* (1973) decision striking down federal and state regulation and prohibition of abortions, and the opinion handed down in *Furman* v *Georgia* (1972) unplugging the electric chairs, are not exactly edicts of a "conservative" bench.

While recognizing for the first time the doctrine of executive privilege, the Burger court also limited this exercise to the area of domestic litigation, holding that in criminal cases the president—*even the president who appointed four of its members*—may be subpoenaed to produce evidence in a criminal trial.

On the traditional side, however, is the decision (*Milligan* v *Bradley*, 1974) that buses transporting school children for the purpose of achieving integration must stop at the Detroit city limits.

The Nixon-Burger court will probably never wear the ultraliberal mantle of the Warren court, but it has demonstrated an independence and a sometimes sense of social awareness which has surprised many observers. History will watch its future decisions with considerable interest.

The Supreme Court has come a long way from the days of John Jay, its first chief justice. Today, when its gavel sounds, the reverberation is felt in every home and industry and institution in the land. The Court can tell people what movies they can see and what books they may read. It can prohibit prayer in public schools (*Engel* v *Vitale*, 1962). Perhaps the ultimate was reached in this land of freedom in 1942 when the Court, applying the commerce clause, told an Ohio farmer that he could not raise more than his AAA allotment of wheat even when every grain of that illegal wheat was consumed on the farm (*Wickard* v *Filburn*).

In today's complex world the United States Constitution is, for better or for worse, whatever the Supreme Court says it is. And if the Supreme Court, in the words of Finley Peter Dunne's Mr. Dooley, "keeps one eye on th' illiction rayturns," maybe the man in the voter's booth has more clout than he thinks he has.

Is each of the following statements true or false?

_____ 1. The Warren court was best known for its landmark decisions in cases involving property rights.

_____ 2. The 1954 school segregation decision was very controversial and has had a profound impact on American life.

_____ 3. The *Baker* v *Carr* case is one of the most far-reaching decisions in American political history.

_____ 4. The Supreme Court has been held in high regard by almost all citizens since the days of John Marshall.

_____ 5. The Burger court, in its early decisions, clearly reflects the philosophy of Richard Nixon, who appointed four of its justices.

Now turn to Answer frame 3[6] on page 78 and check your responses.

Answer frame 3⁶

1. False. It was known for its landmark decisions in cases involving *human values*.
2. True. It was (and still is) very controversial and has brought about many changes involving integration of the races.
3. True. It ruled that state legislative apportionment must be according to "one man, one vote." Many state legislatures had been disproportionately controlled by their rural areas. This decision created a new ruling class in many states.
4. False. The liberals are unhappy with the Court when it is composed of conservatives and vice versa. If we agree with its decisions we tend to hold the Court in high regard; if not, we tend to condemn it, using phrases such as those "nine old men."
5. False. The Burger court, although more conservative than the Warren Court, has handed down "liberal" decisions on abortion and capital punishment, and has even ruled against Mr. Nixon on a matter of "executive privilege."

If you missed any of the above, reread Frame 3⁶.

appendix A

Introduction to the Declaration of Independence

"Most noble document ever conceived by the mind of man"

The city of Quebec in 1759 was a natural fortress fashioned by God, reinforced by the French, and garrisoned by the troops of the Marquis de Montcalm. From his command post on the Plains of Abraham, high above the city, the intrepid Montcalm could look down upon the St. Lawrence Valley and smile with a comfort born of military wisdom. From this superb tactical position, his defending French forces were secure from any threat of the British General James Wolfe, whose forces numbered about 7,000.

But the 33 year old British commander apparently did not understand the meaning of the word "impossible." Under cover of darkness his boats slithered 3,600 men down the St. Lawrence to a point from which they would be able to negotiate the rugged ascent to the Plains. At daybreak on September 13 the French awakened to find the Wolfe at their doorstep. In the fierce fighting, which raged for several days, both generals lost their lives. Montcalm's last hours were rendered even more bitter by the sense of impending defeat; Wolfe's were comforted in the radiance of historic victory.

The fall of Quebec City was the climax of the French and Indian War. A few weeks later Admiral Hawke destroyed a large French fleet off the coast of Brittany; Montreal would fall within 12 months. The French menace in America was forever eradicated.

The French and Indian War in the New World was but a sideshow in the global Seven Years War (1756–63) which climaxed the century-long confrontation between two rising European powers—France and England. The struggle for dominion in Africa would simmer into the 19th century. On the European front, Prussia's Frederick the Great, bankrolled by his English allies, delivered devastating blows to the French land forces. In India, the legendary Robert Clive spearheaded a drive for English hegemony. His brilliant military triumph in 1757 gave the English mastery of Bengal; Pondicherry, the French capital in India, crumbled in 1761. Between his unsuccessful suicide attempt as a teenager and his successful attempt as a middle-age man, the clerk who had no formal military experience had conquered one of the most lucrative empires in world history.

Her status as an international commercial power severely dimmed, her ships swept from the high seas, her African visions frustrated, her colonial empires in America and India destroyed, her land forces humiliated at home, her treasury emptied, France came out of the Seven Years War and the calamitous Treaty of Paris of 1763 with a bitterness toward England that was as deep as the Channel which separated the two neighbors.

It was a venom which would soon steer the rudder of history. For it was consuming contempt for the British more than friendship for America which motivated the bankrupt and downtrodden French to provide the critical arms and supplies which 20 years later would prove decisive in America's War of Independence.

Our forefathers' disenchantment with the mother country intensified shortly after the French threat was dispelled. How natural, thought George III and his Parliament, that Americans be asked to defray some of the war-time expenses and part of the continuing cost of maintaining British soldiers to keep the peace along the Ohio Valley. In arbitrarily imposing taxes for these purposes, the English incited the first successful revolution in the history of modern Western Civilization.

George III, Lord North, Lord Townshend, the Stamp Act, the Intolerable Acts, the Stamp Act Congress, the Declaratory Act, the Sugar Act, the Writs of Assistance, the Boston Tea Party, the Continental Congress, Concord, Lexington, Minute Men, *Common Sense*, the midnight ride of Paul Revere "give me liberty or give me death" and "taxation without representation is tyranny": these are but a few of the familiar notes in the overture that introduced the Declaration of Independence to centerstage in world history. They were notes orchestrated in the stirring, quickstep years from the fall of Quebec (1759) to that Fourth Day of July 1776, when a new nation would forsake the womb of the mother country and take its first shaky steps on its own.

It was to this pulsing background that Richard Henry Lee a delegate from Virginia rose in the Second Continental Congress on June 7, 1776, and proposed three resolutions, the first of which pronounced that:

these United Colonies are, and of right ought to be, free and independent States, that they are absolved from all allegiance to the British Crown, and that all political connection between them and the State of Great Britain is, and ought to be, totally dissolved.

Several of the state delegations believed they were without authority to cast votes on such a crucial question, and a postponement of several weeks was agreed upon. Three days later the Congress voted to appoint a committee to prepare a statement of reasons for such a breakaway, to be announced to the world in event Congress passed the resolution of the honorable gentleman from Virginia. The following day, June 11, a

committee was named, consisting of Thomas Jefferson, John Adams, Benjamin Franklin, Roger Sherman, and Robert Livingston.

The task of authorship providentially fell upon Thomas Jefferson, "the man whom God would have selected to compose the Sermon on the Mount, had he been around at the time." Aristocratic yet democratic, firm but tolerant, possessed of the mind of a scholar and the heart of a humanist, the tall, ruddy, 33 year old Virginia bluestocking was a masterful choice to translate into clear, logical perspective the spirit of rebellion, the wisdom of the *philosophes,* and the mortal sins of George III.

Lawyer, assemblyman, congressman, violinist, horseman, architect, inventor, educator, writer, country squire, patron of art, Jefferson had an enthusiasm for literature, political science, geology, zoology, medicine, and aeronautics that was matched by an intense lifelong interest in democracy, the common welfare, human rights, and dignity. He was not new to the job. From his sickbed he had drafted Virginia's defiant reply to Lord North's "propositions." In 1775, as a congressman, he wrote Congress' answer to those same propositions, as well as the Congressional "Declaration of the Causes and Necessity for Taking up Arms." He also was author of a pamphlet, A *Summary View of the Rights of Americans* (1774), in which he posed cogent historical precedents which questioned the English Parliament's legal claim to authority over colonial America.

The record shows that this flaming interest in basic constitutional rights did not dim after July 4, 1776. In 1788, while serving as minister to France, his would be one of the most strident voices insisting upon a Bill of Rights to accompany the Constitution. Twenty-two years after the Declaration of Independence was adopted, Jefferson would be in the forefront of the fight to repeal the freedom-destroying Alien and Sedition Acts. In this campaign the two most effective instruments were the Virginia and Kentucky Resolutions. He lent his prestige to adoption of the Virginia Resolutions and was author of the Kentucky Resolutions. No man in America was better fitted, philosophically and intellectually, to write the "most noble document ever conceived by the mind of man."

Working long hours at the portable folding desk which he himself had designed (and which is now on display at the National Museum, Washington), Jefferson came up with an initial draft which he submitted to Adams and Franklin. After incorporating their suggestions for changes, he presented the statement (the word "Declaration" was never used by Jefferson at that time) to the committee, which recommended further amendments. On June 28 the committee submitted the approved draft to the Continental Congress, which in turn insisted on numerous modifications. To Jefferson, the most distasteful of these was the deletion of the statement condemning the slave trade.

Richard Henry Lee's Resolution of Independence was adopted by Congress on *July 2, 1776, a day that might logically have been designated as the birthday of our Republic.*

But History had its eye on another day and a more stirring document. On July 4 the Congress approved Jefferson's statement of the reasons compelling the colonists to adopt Lee's Resolution. It was this statement that was later christened the Declaration of Independence.

An historic document, the English Bill of Rights, and a famous political tract, John Locke's *Second Treatise of Government*, were Jefferson's primary sources for the Declaration of Independence.

In 1688, fearing a Catholic succession, the Whigs accomplished their Glorious Revolution, overthrowing James II and bringing William of Orange and Mary (James' Protestant daughter by a first marriage) to the English throne. In consequence of this, the world-famous Bill of Rights was adopted the following year, guaranteeing the Protestant succession for all time, listing basic constitutional rights, and detailing the charges against James II.

The causes which prompted the Whigs to rebel against James Stuart in 1688 were much the same as those which motivated the American colonists to revolt against George III a century later. Jefferson pounced on this remarkable political parallel. His litany of accusations against George III are in the same vein as the 13 charges which the English made against their own king shortly after they forced him to flee to France, tossing the Great Seal in the Thames on his escape to safety. "By God, they are paddling us with our own belt straps," remarked one of the Lords in Parliament upon reading the American Declaration of Independence. It is interesting to note that Jefferson fixed total blame upon George III. The word "Parliament" is never mentioned in the Declaration.

Chief political and philosophical apologist for the English action in dethroning James II was John Locke, 1632–1704, whose first and second *Treatises of Government* (1690) were written to justify the Glorious Revolution. His theories of a "compact system of government," of a "social contract," and of the "right to rebellion," detailed in *The Second Treatise of Government*, were copied by Jefferson in the Declaration of Independence.

Men enter the world totally free, according to Locke. They are unfettered by any chains of authority and endowed by their Creator with such "natural" rights as life, liberty, and property. But because of the imperfections of man, the state of total serenity and security in nature is not attainable without a few "ground rules." Thus, men voluntarily surrender a part of their freedom in order to protect their lives and possessions. By agreement (or compact) they choose a way of government headed by one of their own. When this compact is broken, the people have not only the right, but the *duty*, to rebel.

James' real sin was having produced a son (the unquestioned heir apparent to the English throne) by his Catholic wife. His official sin was "having endeavoured to subvert the constitution of the kingdom by breaking the original contract between king and people, and having, by the advice of Jesuits and other wicked persons, violated the fundamental laws. . . ."

Theorists also read into the Declaration the "social contract" ideas of Rousseau, the "natural law" doctrines of Aquinas and other medievalists, the admonitions of Thomas Paine as expressed in *Common Sense,* and some of the thinking of Montesquieu, Grotius, and even Plato. Although the sage of Monticello was familiar with the works of all these men, and others, John Locke remains the philosophical seed from which the Declaration of Independence sprouted.

Although reference in this chapter is primarily to the English revolt of 1688, it must be remembered that the first 60 years of the 17th century was a running chronicle of the constitutional conflict which raged between crown and Parliament in England. Many of the constitutional points brought home by Jefferson and others in the 1770s were the same as those propounded by Sir Edmund Coke, John Pym, John Hampden, John Milton, and by Oliver Cromwell and his Roundheads as they sent Charles II to his eternal reward in 1649.

There are three "official" texts of the Declaration—the "rough draft," the "corrected" version, and the familiar copy, engrossed on parchment with the signatures, headed by the bold autograph of John Hancock.

The "rough draft" broadside was printed by John Dunlap of Philadelphia a few hours after the Declaration was approved. This is the text first authorized to be printed by Congress and the one inserted in the "rough" Journal of Congress.

The "corrected" text is in the handwriting of Charles Thomson, secretary of Congress, and is placed in the "corrected" Journal of Congress.

Both of these texts are preserved in the papers of the Continental Congress in the Library of Congress.

The parchment copy, preserved in a helium-filled glass, is the familiar one displayed in countless photographs and viewed annually by millions of visitors who throng the National Archives Building in Washington, D.C.

The first celebration of the Declaration of Independence took place July 8, 1776, at Independence Hall (known then as the state house). The celebrators were summoned for a reading by the pealing of the Liberty Bell. The story that the Liberty Bell first cracked on that day has been widely circulated, but is untrue. It cracked for the first time in 1752 after being brought from London.

In the annals of world history, few documents have had such enormous influence. The words of the Declaration of Independence were the inspiration for French patriots who revolted against 200 years of Bourbon oppression in 1789 to proclaim their own *Declaration of the Rights of Man and of the Citizen*. In the years from 1789 to 1848 numerous revolutionary movements erupted throughout Europe; between 1810 and 1825 virtually every country in South America rose in protest. Wherever men have risked their lives to rid themselves of the burden of unjust government, Jefferson's ringing statement of America's revolutionary rationale has stood out like a beacon of hope in the canyon of royal absolutism.

Thomas Jefferson died on July 4, 1826, at Monticello on the golden anniversary of the Declaration of Independence, within hours of the death of another great patriot, John Adams. Thus, the bicentennial anniversary of the Declaration of Independence will fall on the sequicentennial anniversary of the death of Adams and Jefferson.

The Declaration of Independence*

In CONGRESS, July 4, 1776
A DECLARATION
By the REPRESENTATIVES of the
UNITED STATES OF AMERICA
In GENERAL CONGRESS assembled

WHEN in the Course of human Events, it becomes necessary for one People to dissolve the Political Bands which have connected them with another, and to assume among the Powers of the Earth, the separate and equal Station to which the Laws of Nature and of Nature's God entitle them, a decent Respect to the Opinions of Mankind requires that they should declare the causes which impel them to the Separation.

WE hold these Truths to be self-evident, that all Men are created equal, that they are endowed by their Creator with certain unalienable Rights, that among these are Life, Liberty, and the Pursuit of Happiness—That to secure these Rights, Governments are instituted among Men, deriving their just Powers from the Consent of the

---

* Text and notes as found in *The Declaration of Independence and The Constitution of the United States of America* (Washington, D.C.: House of Representatives, 1964), pp. 1–5.

Governed, that whenever any Form of Government becomes destructive of these Ends, it is the Right of the People to alter or to abolish it, and to institute new Government, laying its Foundation on such Principles, and organizing its Powers in such Form, as to them shall seem most likely to effect their Safety and Happiness. Prudence, indeed, will dictate that Governments long established should not be changed for light and transient Causes; and accordingly all Experience hath shewn, that Mankind are more disposed to suffer, while Evils are sufferable, than to right themselves by abolishing the Forms to which they are accustomed. But when a long Train of Abuses and Usurpations, pursuing invariably the same Object, evinces a Design to reduce them under absolute Despotism, it is their Right, it is their duty, to throw off such Government, and to provide new Guards for their future Security. Such has been the patient Sufferance of these Colonies; and such is now the Necessity which constrains them to alter their former Systems of Government. The History of the present King of Great-Britain is a History of repeated Injuries and Usurpations, all having in direct Object the Establishment of an absolute Tyranny over these States. To prove this, let Facts be submitted to a candid World.

He has refused his Assent to Laws, the most wholesome and necessary for the public Good.

He has forbidden his Governors to pass Laws of immediate and pressing Importance, unless suspended in their Operation till his Assent should be obtained; and when so suspended, he has utterly neglected to attend to them.

He has refused to pass other Laws for the Accommodation of large Districts of People, unless those People would relinquish the Right of Representation in the Legislature, a Right inestimable to them, and formidable to Tyrants only.

He has called together Legislative Bodies at Places unusual, uncomfortable, and distant from the Depository of their public Records, for the sole Purpose of fatiguing them into Compliance with his Measures.

He has dissolved Representative Houses repeatedly, for opposing with manly Firmness his Invasions on the Rights of the People.

He has refused for a long Time, after such Dissolutions, to cause others to be elected; whereby the Legislative Powers, incapable of Annihilation, have returned to the People at large for their exercise; the State remaining in the mean time exposed to all the Dangers of Invasion from without, and Convulsions within.

He has endeavoured to prevent the Population of these States; for that Purpose obstructing the Laws for Naturalization of Foreigners; refusing to pass others to encourage their Migrations hither, and raising the Conditions of new Appropriations of Lands.

He has obstructed the Administration of Justice, by refusing his Assent to Laws for establishing Judiciary Powers.

He has made Judges dependent on his Will alone, for the Tenure of their Offices, and the Amount and Payment of their Salaries.

He has erected a Multitude of new Offices, and sent hither Swarms of Officers to harrass our People, and eat out their Substance.

He has kept among us, in Times of Peace, Standing Armies, without the consent of our Legislatures.

He has affected to render the Military independent of and superior to the Civil Power.

He has combined with others to subject us to a Jurisdiction foreign to our Constitution, and unacknowledged by our Laws; giving his Assent to their Acts of pretended Legislation:

For quartering large Bodies of Armed Troops among us:

For protecting them, by a mock Trial, from Punishment for any Murders which they should commit on the Inhabitants of these States:

For cutting off our Trade with all Parts of the World:

For imposing Taxes on us without our Consent:

For depriving us, in many Cases, of the Bene fits of Trial by Jury:

For transporting us beyond Seas to be tried for pretended Offences:

For abolishing the free System of English Laws in a neighboring Province, establishing therein an arbitrary Government, and enlarging its Boundaries, so as to render it at once an Example and fit Instrument for introducing the same absolute Rule into these Colonies:

For taking away our Charters, abolishing our

most valuable Laws, and altering fundamentally the Forms of our Governments:

FOR suspending our own Legislatures, and declaring themselves invested with Power to legislate for us in all Cases whatsoever.

HE has abdicated Government here, by declaring us out of his Protection and waging War against us.

HE has plundered our Seas, ravaged our Coasts, burnt our Towns, and destroyed the Lives of our People.

HE is, at this Time, transporting large Armies of foreign Mercenaries to compleat the Works of Death, Desolation, and Tyranny, already begun with circumstances of Cruelty and Perfidy, scarcely paralleled in the most barbarous Ages, and totally unworthy the Head of a civilized Nation.

HE has constrained our fellow Citizens taken Captive on the high Seas to bear Arms against their Country, to become the Executioners of their Friends and Brethren, or to fall themselves at their Hands.

HE has excited domestic Insurrections amongst us, and has endeavoured to bring on the Inhabitants of our Frontiers, the merciless Indian Savages, whose known Rule of Warfare, is an undistinguished Destruction, of all Ages, Sexes and Conditions.

IN every stage of these Oppressions we have Petitioned for Redress in the most humble Terms: Our repeated Petitions have been answered only by repeated Injury. A Prince, whose Character is thus marked by every act which may define a Tyrant, is unfit to be the Ruler of a free People.

NOR have we been wanting in Attentions to our British Brethren. We have warned them from Time to Time of Attempts by their Legislature to extend an unwarrantable Jurisdiction over us. We have reminded them of the Circumstances of our Emigration and Settlement here. We have appealed to their native Justice and Magnanimity, and we have conjured them by the Ties of our common Kindred to disavow these Usurpations, which, would inevitably interrupt our Connections and Correspondence. They too have been deaf to the Voice of Justice and of Consanguinity. We must, therefore, acquiesce in the Necessity, which denounces our Separation, and hold them, as we hold the rest of Mankind, Enemies in War, in Peace, Friends.

WE, therefore, the Representatives of the UNITED STATES OF AMERICA, in GENERAL CONGRESS, Assembled, appealing to the Supreme Judge of the World for the Rectitude of our Intentions, do, in the Name, and by Authority of the good People of these Colonies, solemnly Publish and Declare, That these United Colonies are, and of Right ought to be, FREE AND INDEPENDENT STATES; that they are absolved from all Allegiance to the British Crown, and that all political Connection between them and the State of Great-Britain, is and ought to be totally dissolved; and that as FREE AND INDEPENDENT STATES, they have full Power to levy War, conclude Peace, contract Alliances, establish Commerce, and to do all other Acts and Things which INDEPENDENT STATES may of right do. And for the support of this Declaration, with a firm Reliance on the Protection of divine Providence, we mutually pledge to each other our Lives, our Fortunes, and our sacred Honor.

Signed by ORDER *and in* BEHALF
of the CONGRESS,
JOHN HANCOCK, PRESIDENT.

ATTEST.
CHARLES THOMSON, SECRETARY.

PHILADELPHIA: PRINTED BY JOHN DUNLAP.

SIGNERS OF THE DECLARATION OF INDEPENDENCE

ACCORDING TO THE AUTHENTICATED LIST PRINTED BY
ORDER OF CONGRESS OF JANUARY 18, 1777*

John Hancock.

NEW-HAMPSHIRE.
{ *Josiah Bartlett,*
W^m. Whipple,
Matthew Thornton.† }

DELAWARE.
{ *Cæsar Rodney,*
Geo. Read,
(Tho M:Kean.)‡ }

MASSACHUSETTS-BAY.
{ *Saml. Adams,*
John Adams,
Robt. Treat Paine,
Elbridge Gerry. }

MARYLAND.
{ *Samuel Chase,*
W^m. Paca,
Thos. Stone,
Charles Carroll, of Carrollton. }

RHODE-ISLAND AND PROVIDENCE, &C.
{ *Step. Hopkins,*
William Ellery. }

CONNECTICUT.
{ *Roger Sherman,*
Saml. Huntington,
W^m. Williams,
Oliver Wolcott. }

VIRGINIA.
{ *George Wythe,*
Richard Henry Lee,
Th^s. Jefferson,
Benj^a. Harrison,
Thos. Nelson, j^r.
Francis Lightfoot Lee,
Carter Braxton. }

NEW-YORK.
{ *W^m. Floyd,*
Phil. Livingston,
Fran^s. Lewis,
Lewis Morris. }

NORTH-CAROLINA.
{ *W^m. Hooper,*
Joseph Hewes,
John Penn. }

NEW-JERSEY.
{ *Rich^d. Stockton,*
Jno. Witherspoon,
Fra^s. Hopkinson,
John Hart,
Abra. Clark. }

SOUTH-CAROLINA.
{ *Edward Rutledge,*
Thos. Heyward, jun^r.
Thomas Lynch, jun^r.
Arthur Middleton. }

PENNSYLVANIA.
{ *Robt. Morris,*
Benjamin Rush,
Benja. Franklin,
John Morton,
Geo. Clymer,
Ja^s. Smith,
Geo. Taylor,
James Wilson,
Geo. Ross. }

GEORGIA.
{ *Button Gwinnett,*
Lyman Hall,
Geo. Walton. }

---

* Braces, spelling, and abbreviation of names conform to original printed list.

† Matthew Thornton's name was signed on the engrossed copy following the Connecticut Members, but was transferred in the printed copy to its proper place with the other New Hampshire Members.

‡ Thomas McKean's name was not included in the list of signers printed by order of Congress on January 18, 1777, as he did not sign the engrossed copy until some time thereafter, probably in 1781.

appendix B

The Articles of Confederation

Introduction

A backdrop of bitterness, fear, and suspicion clouds the phraseology and philosophy of the Articles of Confederation. Forged in the flames of war, the document is dominated by a fierce resolve to cling to a local type of autonomy but tempered by a grudging realization that it is better to hang together than to hang separately.

In July of 1775, while the memory of Concord and Lexington was still fresh, Benjamin Franklin proposed to the Continental Congress a plan for "Articles of Confederation and Perpetual Union." But Franklin's "firm league of friendship" was dismissed; the colonists were not yet ready to grant to any government—even one of their own formation—a slice of that political independence which many of them would soon defend with their lives.

On June 7, 1777 Richard Henry Lee's resolution for a Declaration of Independence was accompanied by a resolution that Congress consider a written constitution. The move carried and John Dickenson headed the committee which reported back on July 12. Conflicts instantly flared between small-states people and large-states people, between nationalists and localists, between idealists and realists.

Dickenson's much debated and embroidered Articles of Confederation were submitted to the states in November 1777, at the beginning of the winter of Valley Forge. Twelve states ratified within two years, but a lone dissenter held up the necessary unanimous approval for another two years. Maryland was disturbed by the claims of seven states—claims which in some cases stretched to the Mississippi and in others length-

Introduction (cont.)

ened to the Pacific. Only when all claims were ceded to the United States did Maryland ratify the Articles and make them the law of the land. In many respects the document merely gave legal, written sanction to a form of government which had been in existence for several years.

The Articles of Confederation, of course, are best known for what they failed to say. Note the absence of a federal judiciary, the lack of a federal taxing authority, the failure to grant the government the power to create its own army or to regulate commerce, and the cavernous void brought about by refusal to name an executive.

Missing also are the graceful prose and simple clarity of the United States Constitution; nor is there any hint of the poetic cadence with which Thomas Jefferson endowed the Declaration of Independence. Details of the various Articles are ponderously qualified, and verbs have a habit of straying word-miles away from their nouns. We challenge the reader, within a 30 minute time limitation, to come up with a meaningful translation of the second sentence of the second paragraph of Article Nine.

Articles of Confederation

To ALL to whom these Presents shall come, we the undersigned Delegates of the States affixed to our Names send greeting.

Whereas the Delegates of the United States of America in Congress assembled did on the fifteenth day of November in the Year of our Lord One Thousand Seven Hundred and Seventy seven, and in the Second Year of the Independence of America agree to certain articles of Confederation and perpetual Union between the States of Newhampshire, Massachusetts-bay, Rhodeisland and Providence Plantations, Connecticut, New York, New Jersey, Pennsylvania, Delaware, Maryland, Virginia, North-Carolina, South-Carolina and Georgia in the Words following, viz.

Articles of Confederation and perpetual Union between the States of Newhampshire, Massachusetts-bay, Rhodeisland and Providence

THE ARTICLES

Plantations, Connecticut, New-York, New-Jersey, Pennsylvania, Delaware, Maryland, Virginia, North-Carolina, South-Carolina and Georgia.

ARTICLE I. The stile of this confederacy shall be "The United States of America."

ARTICLE II. Each State retains its sovereignty, freedom and independence, and every power, jurisdiction and right, which is not by this confederation expressly delegated to the United States, in Congress assembled.

ARTICLE III. The said States hereby severally enter into a firm league of friendship with each other, for their common defence, the security of their liberties, and their mutual and general welfare, binding themselves to assist each other, against all force offered to, or attacks made upon them, or any of them, on account of religion, sovereignty, trade, or any other pretence whatever.

ARTICLE IV. The better to secure and perpetuate mutual friendship and intercourse among the people of the different States in this Union, the free inhabitants of each of these States, paupers, vagabonds and fugitives from justice excepted, shall be entitled to all privileges and immunities of free citizens in the several States; and the people of each State shall have free ingress and regress to and from any other State, and shall enjoy therein all the privileges of trade and commerce, subject to the same duties, impositions and restrictions as the inhabitants thereof respectively, provided that such restrictions shall not extend so far as to prevent the removal of property imported into any State, to any other State of which the owner is an inhabitant; provided also that no imposition, duties or restriction shall be laid by any State, on the property of the United States, or either of them.

If any person guilty of, or charged with treason, felony, or other high misdemeanor in any State, shall flee from justice, and be found in any of the United States, he shall upon demand of the Governor or Executive power, of the State

Explanations and Comments

This Article, a total victory for the states' rights faction, sets the pattern for the entire Articles. Clearly, the majority wished to guard against a strong central government. If they were successful in breaking away from the authority of George III and Parliament, they meant to insure they would never again be so dominated.

Note the terms *firm league of friendship, common defence,* and *security of their liberties.* Following the tone struck in Article II, Article III's statement of purpose indicates that the Articles of Confederation were conceived primarily as a mutual alliance in the fight against England. As much autonomy as possible would be reserved for the individual states.

Some are more equal than others.

States were free to impose duties on interstate commerce. A windfall for New York. (One of the main faults of the Articles.)

THE ARTICLES (cont.)

from which he fled, be delivered up and removed to the State having jurisdiction of his offence.

Full faith and credit shall be given in each of these States to the records, acts and judicial proceedings of the courts and magistrates of every other State.

ARTICLE V. For the more convenient management of the general interests of the United States, delegates shall be annually appointed in such manner as the legislature of each State shall direct, to meet in Congress on the first Monday in November, in every year, with a power reserved to each State, to recall its delegates, or any of them, at any time within the year, and to send others in their stead, for the remainder of the year.

No State shall be represented in Congress by less than two, nor by more than seven members; and no person shall be capable of being a delegate for more than three years in any term of six years; nor shall any person, being a delegate, be capable of holding any office under the United States, for which he, or another for his benefit receives any salary, fees or emolument of any kind.

Each State shall maintain its own delegates in a meeting of the States, and while they act as members of the committee of the States.

In determining questions in the United States, in Congress assembled, each State shall have one vote.

Freedom of speech and debate in Congress shall not be impeached or questioned in any court, or place out of Congress, and the members of Congress shall be protected in their persons from arrests and imprisonments, during the time of their going to and from, and attendance on Congress, except for treason, felony, or breach of the peace.

ARTICLE VI. No State without the consent of the United States in Congress assembled, shall end any embassy to, or receive any embassy from, or enter into any conference, agreement, alliance or treaty with any king, prince or state; nor shall any person holding any office of profit or trust under the United States, or any of them, accept of any present, emolument, office or

Explanations and Comments

Paragraph 3 was lifted almost verbatim by the authors of the Constitution. In both documents, extradition and full faith and credit are dealt with in Article IV.

Note: A *single* legislative branch; members appointed *annually* with each state free to select the manner in which delegates would be chosen. Annual appointments reflected the colonists revulsion against a House-of-Lords-type rule where peers were elected for life.

Paragraph 2. Since the states paid the delegates, each state could have as many as it wished; however, each state got only one vote.

Again, the Articles carefully guard against long terms of office.

Paragraph 4. Total victory for the small states. Delaware could exert the same power as Massachusetts or Pennsylvania.

Article VI. Prohibitions on the states.

THE ARTICLES (cont.)

title of any kind whatever from any king, prince or foreign state; nor shall the United States in Congress assembled, or any of them, grant any title of nobility.

No two or more States shall enter into any treaty, confederation or alliance whatever between them, without the consent of the United States in Congress assembled, specifying accurately the purposes for which the same is to be entered into, and how long it shall continue.

No State shall lay any imposts or duties, which may interfere with any stipulations in treaties, entered into by the United States in Congress assembled, with any king, prince or state, in pursuance of any treaties already proposed by Congress, to the courts of France and Spain.

No vessels of war shall be kept up in time of peace by any State, except such number only, as shall be deemed necessary by the United States in Congress assembled, for the defence of such State, or its trade; nor shall any body of forces be kept up by any State, in time of peace, except such number only, as in the judgment of the United States, in Congress assembled, shall be deemed requisite to garrison the forts necessary for the defence of such State; but every State shall always keep up a well regulated and disciplined militia, sufficiently armed and accoutred, and shall provide and constantly have ready for use, in public stores, a due number of field pieces and tents, and a proper quantity of arms, ammunition and camp equipage.

No State shall engage in any war without the consent of the United States in Congress assembled, unless such State be actually invaded by enemies, or shall have received certain advice of a resolution being formed by some nation of Indians to invade such State, and the danger is so imminent as not to admit of a delay, till the United States in Congress assembled can be consulted: nor shall any State grant commissions to any ships or vessels of war, nor letters of marque or reprisal, except it be after a declaration of war by the United States in Congress assembled, and then only against the kingdom or state and the subjects thereof, against which war has been so declared, and under such regulations as shall be established by the United States in Congress assembled, unless such State

Explanations and Comments

Paragraph 1. Expressing a common revulsion against the British system.

THE ARTICLES (cont.)

be infested by pirates, in which case vessels of war may be fitted out for that occasion, and kept so long as the danger shall continue, or until the United States in Congress assembled shall determine otherwise.

ARTICLE VII. When land-forces are raised by any State for the common defence, all officers of or under the rank of colonel, shall be appointed by the Legislature of each State respectively by whom such forces shall be raised, or in such manner as such State shall direct, and all vacancies shall be filled up by the State which first made the appointment.

ARTICLE VIII. All charges of war, and all other expenses that shall be incurred for the common defence or general welfare, and allowed by the United States in Congress assembled, shall be defrayed out of a common treasury, which shall be supplied by the several States, in proportion to the value of all land within each State, granted to or surveyed for any person, as such land and the buildings and improvements thereon shall be estimated according to such mode as the United States in Congress assembled, shall from time to time direct and appoint.

The taxes for paying that proportion shall be laid and levied by the authority and direction of the Legislatures of the several States within the time agreed upon by the United States in Congress assembled.

ARTICLE IX. The United States in Congress assembled, shall have the sole and exclusive right and power of determining on peace and war, except in the cases mentioned in the sixth article—of sending and receiving ambassadors—entering into treaties and alliances, provided that no treaty of commerce shall be made whereby the legislative power of the respective States shall be restrained from imposing such imposts and duties on foreigners, as their own people are subjected to, or from prohibiting the exportation or importation of any species of goods or commodities whatsoever—of establishing rules for deciding all cases, what captures on land or water shall be legal, and in what manner prizes taken by land or naval forces in the service of the United States shall be divided or

Explanations and Comments

Article VIII.

The good intentions expressed in Articles VII and VIII are nullified by this ambiguous and unenforceable clause. Again, the individual state legislatures exerted enormous power.

Article IX. The legislative authority.

THE ARTICLES (cont.)

appropriated—of granting letters of marque and reprisal in times of peace—appointing courts for the trial of piracies and felonies committed on the high seas and establishing courts for receiving and determining finally appeals in all cases of captures, provided that no member of Congress shall be appointed a judge of any of the said courts.

The United States in Congress assembled shall also be the last resort on appeal in all disputes and differences now subsisting or that hereafter may arise between two or more States concerning boundary, jurisdiction or any other cause whatever; which authority shall always be exercised in the manner following. Whenever the legislative or executive authority or lawful agent of any State in controversy with another shall present a petition to Congress, stating the matter in question and praying for a hearing, notice thereof shall be given by order of Congress to the legislative or executive authority of the other State in controversy, and a day assigned for the appearance of the parties by their lawful agents, who shall then be directed to appoint by joint consent, commissioners or judges to constitute a court for hearing and determining the matter in question: but if they cannot agree, Congress shall name three persons out of each of the United States, and from the list of such persons each party shall alternately strike out one, the petitioners beginning, until the number shall be reduced to thirteen; and from that number not less than seven, nor more than nine names as Congress shall direct, shall in the presence of Congress be drawn out by lot, and the persons whose names shall be so drawn or any five of them, shall be commissioners or judges, to hear and finally determine the controversy, so always as a major part of the judges who shall hear the cause shall agree in the determination: and if either party shall neglect to attend at the day appointed, without showing reasons, which Congress shall judge sufficient, or being present shall refuse to strike, the Congress shall proceed to nominate three persons out of each State, and the Secretary of Congress shall strike in behalf of such party absent or refusing; and the judgment and sentence of the court to be appointed, in the manner be-

THE ARTICLES (cont.)

fore prescribed, shall be final and conclusive; and if any of the parties shall refuse to submit to the authority of such court, or to appear or defend their claim or cause, the court shall nevertheless proceed to pronounce sentence, or judgment, which shall in like manner be final or decisive, the judgment or sentence and other proceedings being in either case transmitted to Congress, and lodged among the acts of Congress for the security of the parties concerned: provided that every commissioner, before he sits in judgment, shall take an oath to be administered by one of the judges of the supreme or superior court of the State where the cause shall be tried, "well and truly to hear and determine the matter in question, according to the best of his judgment, without favour, affection or hope of reward:" provided also that no State shall be deprived of territory for the benefit of the United States.

All controversies concerning the private right of soil claimed under different grants of two or more States, whose jurisdiction as they may respect such lands, and the States which passed such grants are adjusted, the said grants or either of them being at the same time claimed to have originated antecedent to such settlement of jurisdiction, shall on the petition of either party to the Congress of the United States, be finally determined as near as may be in the same manner as is before prescribed for deciding disputes respecting territorial jurisdiction between different States.

The United States in Congress assembled shall also have the sole and exclusive right and power of regulating the alloy and value of coin struck by their own authority, or by that of the respective States—fixing the standard of weights and measures throughout the United States—regulating the trade and managing all affairs with the Indians, not members of any of the States, provided that the legislative right of any State within its own limits be not infringed or violated—establishing and regulating post-offices from one State to another, throughout all the United States, and exacting such postage on the papers passing thro' the same as may be requisite to defray the expenses of the said office—appointing all officers of the land forces, in the service of the United States, excepting regimen-

THE ARTICLES (cont.)

tal officers—appointing all the officers of the naval forces, and commissioning all officers whatever in the service of the United States—making rules for the government and regulation of the said land and naval forces, and directing their operations.

The United States in Congress assembled shall have authority to appoint a committee, to sit in the recess of Congress, to be denominated "a Committee of the States," and to consist of one delegate from each State; and to appoint such other committees and civil officers as may be necessary for managing the general affairs of the United States under their direction—to appoint one of their number to preside, provided that no person be allowed to serve in the office of president more than one year in any term of three years; to ascertain the necessary sums of money to be raised for the service of the United States, and to appropriate and apply the same for defraying the public expenses—to borrow money, or emit bills on the credit of the United States, transmitting every half year to the respective States an account of the sums of money so borrowed or emitted,—to build and equip a navy—to agree upon the number of land forces, and to make requisitions from each State for its quota, in proportion to the number of white inhabitants in such State; which requisition shall be binding, and thereupon the Legislature of each State shall appoint the regimental officers, raise the men and cloath, arm and equip them in a soldier like manner, at the expense of the United States; and the officers and men so cloathed, armed and equipped shall march to the place appointed, and within the time agreed on by the United States in Congress assembled: but if the United States in Congress assembled shall, on consideration of circumstances judge proper that any State should not raise men, or should raise a smaller number of men than the quota thereof, such extra number shall be raised, officered, cloathed, armed and equipped in the same manner as the quota of such State, unless the legislature of such State shall judge that such extra number cannot be safely spared out of the same, in which case they shall raise officer, cloath, arm and equip as many of such extra number as they judge can be safely spared. And

Explanations and Comments

One delegate from each state—again, the smallest and poorest state may exert the same political "clout" as its biggest and richest brother state.

This committee was closest thing to an "executive authority." At one time about 100 committees existed, with authorities and functions overlapping and sometimes duplicating.

Congress could only make *requisitions* for troops.

One more indication of the status of blacks.

THE ARTICLES (cont.)

the officers and men so cloathed, armed and equipped, shall march to the place appointed, and within the time agreed on by the United States in Congress assembled.

The United States in Congress assembled shall never engage in a war, nor grant letters of marque and reprisal in time of peace, nor enter into any treaties or alliances, nor coin money, nor regulate the value thereof, nor ascertain the sums and expenses necessary for the defence and welfare of the United States, or any of them, nor emit bills, nor borrow money on the credit of the United States, nor appropriate money, nor agree upon the number of vessels of war, to be built or purchased, or the number of land or sea forces to be raised, nor appoint a commander in chief of the army or navy, unless nine States assent to the same: nor shall a question on any other point, except for adjourning from day to day be determined, unless by the votes of a majority of the United States in Congress assembled.

The Congress of the United States shall have power to adjourn to any time within the year, and to any place within the United States, so that no period of adjournment be for a longer duration than the space of six months, and shall publish the journal of their proceedings monthly, except such parts thereof relating to treaties, alliances or military operations, as in their judgment require secrecy; and the yeas and nays of the delegates of each State on any question shall be entered on the Journal, when it is desired by any delegate; and the delegates of a State, or any of them, at his or their request shall be furnished with a transcript of the said journal, except such parts as are above excepted, to lay before the Legislatures of the several States.

ARTICLE X. The committee of the States, or any nine of them, shall be authorized to execute, in the recess of Congress, such of the powers of Congress as the United States in Congress assembled, by the consent of nine States, shall from time to time think expedient to vest them with; provided that no power be delegated to the said committee, for the exercise of which, by the articles of confederation, the voice of

Explanations and Comments

Paragraph 6. Note that important issues required consent of nine of the states. Five tiny states could thwart the wishes of three fourths of the population of the country. The obtaining of nine consenting votes was made even more difficult by the rule that state delegations which were evenly voted would be officially registered as not voting.

Article X. The extremely cautionate states' rights philosophy is again expressed here. The committee of states can only act with the approval of nine states.

THE ARTICLES (cont.)

nine States in the Congress of the United States assembled is requisite.

ARTICLE XI. Canada acceding to this confederation, and joining in the measures of the United States, shall be admitted into, and entitled to all the advantages of this Union: but no other colony shall be admitted into the same, unless such admission be agreed to by nine States.

ARTICLE XII. All bills of credit emitted, monies borrowed and debts contracted by, or under the authority of Congress, before the assembling of the United States, in pursuance of the present confederation, shall be deemed and considered as a charge against the United States, for payment and satisfaction whereof the said United States, and the public faith are hereby solemnly pledged.

ARTICLE XIII. Every State shall abide by the determinations of the United States in Congress assembled, on all questions which by this confederation are submitted to them. And the articles of this confederation shall be inviolably observed by every State, and the Union shall be perpetual; *nor shall any alteration at any time hereafter be made in any of them; unless such alteration be agreed to in a Congress of the United States, and be afterwards confirmed by the Legislatures of every State.*

And whereas it has pleased the Great Governor of the world to incline the hearts of the Legislatures we respectively represent in Congress, to approve of, and to authorize us to ratify the said articles of confederation and perpetual union. Know ye that we the undersigned delegates, by virtue of the power and authority to us given for that purpose, do by these presents, in the name and in behalf of our respective constituents, fully and entirely ratify and confirm each and every of the said articles of confederation and perpetual union, and all and singular the matters and things therein contained: and we do further solemnly plight and engage the faith of our respective constituents, that they shall abide by the determinations of the United States in Congress assembled, on all questions,

Explanations and Comments

Article XII. Compare with Paragraph 1 of Article VI of the Constitution.

Article XIII. The italicized phrase probably doomed the Articles of Confederation and brought on the present Constitution. Because of the diverse interests, it was virtually impossible to obtain the unanimous consent necessary to amend the Articles. All other faults of the Articles could have been corrected through amendment.

THE ARTICLES (cont.)

which by the said confederation are submitted to them. And that the articles thereof shall be inviolably observed by the States we respectively represent, and that the Union shall be perpetual.

In witness whereof we have hereunto set our hands in Congress. Done at Philadelphia in the State of Pennsylvania the ninth day of July in the year of our Lord one thousand seven hundred and seventy-eight, and in the third year of the independence of America.

Now turn to page 98 to work the sample Constitutional examination.

Sample Constitutional examination

Fill in the blanks

1. Members of the House of Representatives are chosen every _____ year.

2. A Representative must reside in the state in which he is chosen, have been a citizen _____ years, and be _____ years old.

3. A U.S. Senator must be _____ years of age and _____ years a citizen.

4. The Senate is presided over by the _____ _____.

5. The president of the Senate may vote only in case of a _____.

6. The sole power of impeachment rests with the _____, and the power to try impeachments lies with the _____.

7. In case of impeachment of the president, the _____ _____ shall preside at the trial.

8. When a vacancy occurs in the Senate, the _____ _____ appoints someone to fill the office until the next general election.

9. When a vacancy occurs in the House, the _____ _____ issues a _____ _____.

10. All revenue-raising bills originate in the _____.

11. Only the _____ has the power to negotiate a treaty. But a treaty, to become law, must be approved by a _____ vote of the _____.

12. The power to appoint ambassadors and Supreme Court justices is vested in the _____.

Multiple choice

_____ 13. Which one of these powers does NOT belong to the Congress:
a. to lay and collect taxes
b. to establish post offices
c. to interpret the laws
d. to provide and maintain a navy
e. to issue patents
f. to coin money
g. to declare war

_____ 14. An impeached government official is NOT subject to which of these penalties as a result of his impeachment:
a. removal from office
b. fine and imprisonment
c. disqualification from holding further federal offices

_____ 15. Which of these crimes is defined in the Constitution?
a. malfeasance in office
b. treason
c. perjury
d. misappropriation of funds

_____ 16. A federal judge serves for:
a. 6 years
b. 4 years
c. life
d. 10 years
e. until he is 70 years old

_____ 17. The principle of judicial review was established in:
a. *Cohens* v *Virginia*
b. *Brown* v *Board of Education*
c. *Marbury* v *Madison*
d. *Nixon* v *Jaworski*

_____ 18. The federal government must guarantee to each state which kind of government?
a. democratic
b. republican
c. popular
d. representative

_____ 19. Article V provides that amendments may be proposed by conventions called by the state legislatures. How many amendments have been ratified in this manner?
a. 4   b. 22   c. none   d. 1
e. 8   f. 26

_____ 20. To become law, an amendment must be ratified by:
a. two thirds of the states
b. the Congress, and signed by the president
c. three fourths of the state legislatures

_____ 21. Article VI provided that all obligations contracted by the Articles of Confederation government:
a. would be paid in full
b. were not necessarily the obligation of the new government
c. would be paid if approved by the Congress and signed by the president

_____ 22. Which of the following is not listed in Article VI as being among the rules which comprise the supreme law of the land?
a. Constitution
b. executive proclamations
c. treaties
d. laws of the U.S.

_____ 23. Which of the following acts is not defined as treasonous?
a. levying war against the U.S.
b. adhering to the enemies of the U.S.
c. "Bugging" the halls of Congress
d. giving aid and comfort to the enemy

_____ 24. Article VI provided that the Constitution, to become law, must be ratified by how many states?
a. 7   b. 13   c. 9   d. 8

_____ 25. Which one of the following was not provided in Article IV?
a. each state must honor the public acts, records and judicial proceedings of every other state.
b. citizens of any state are entitled to the privileges of citizens of all the states.
c. states must turn over captured criminals who are wanted in other states.
d. states must not harbor runaway slaves from another state.
e. in time of war, states may restrict out-of-state traffic on their roads and waterways.

_____ 26. Nelson Rockefeller and John Lindsay could not run on the same ticket for president and vice president because:
a. Rockefeller is a Republican and Lindsay is a Democrat.
b. both are from the same state.
c. Article II provides that a presidential candidate from the east must have a running mate from another section of the country.

_____ 27. Carmelita Gomez, a Mexican citizen who illegally entered the United States to work and live in a Texas border town, bears a child out of wedlock. The child, according to the 14th Amendment, is therefore:
a. a full-fledged U.S. citizen.
b. considered an alien.
c. possessed of half citizenship if it can be proved the father was a U.S. citizen.

The Bill of Rights

Which amendment am I?

_____ 1. I am the amendment which allows the individual states to form National Guards.

_____ 2. I provide citizens security against unreasonable search and seizure.

_____ 3. In criminal cases, I guarantee a "speedy and public trial by an impartial jury.

_____ 4. I make sure that certain basic, natural rights belong to every citizen, though they may not be specifically listed in the Constitution.

_____ 5. I guarantee a trial by jury in suits at common law where the amount in dispute exceeds $20.00.

_____ 6. I am the Constitutional freedom cited by gangsters who wish to remain silent under courtroom interrogation.

_____ 7. I am the amendment cited by states-righters; I maintain that certain powers not specifically delegated to the federal government and not forbidden to the states *are reserved to the states.*

_____ 8. Because of me, Congress can "make no law abridging the freedom of speech, or of the press."

_____ 9. I prevent the government from forcibly quartering a soldier in a citizen's home.

_____ 10. I protect John Citizen against assessment of excessive bail, imposition of excessive fines, and from cruel and unusual imprisonment.

_____ 11. I provide basic Constitutional rights for the citizen placed under arrest.

_____ 12. Thanks to me, the United States has no national religion, and every citizen is free to worship, or not to worship, without interference.

The Other Amendments

Which amendment:

_____ 1. Might be said to have started women's lib?

_____ 2. Allowed citizens of the District of Columbia the right to vote for president?

_____ 3. Granted immunity to a State against suit in federal court by a citizen of another state?

_____ 4. Gave 18-year-olds the right to vote?

_____ 5. Brought about the direct election of Senators?

_____ 6. Provided for a new and orderly succession in the case of death, resignation or removal from office of the president or vice president?

_____ 7. Was the first of three "Civil War Amendments" dealing with slavery, citizenship and suffrage?

_____ 8. Was passed because Burr almost stole the presidency from Jefferson in the election of 1800?

_____ 9. Brought on the bootlegging era?

_____ 10. Ended the bootlegging era?

_____ 11. Insured that no voter will ever be charged a poll tax in a federal election?

_____ 12. Banned slavery in the U.S.?

_____ 13. Clipped the lame ducks' wings?

_____ 14. Assured that the right to vote may not be abridged because of race, color or previous condition of servitude?

_____ 15. Conferred a new type of *national* citizenship—quite apart from *state* citizenship—and conferred precious civil rights to all citizens?

_____ 16. Insured that no president will ever serve more than two *full* terms?

_____ 17. Legalized the income tax?

Fill in the correct answers

18. The _____ would succeed to the presidency in the event of the death of the president and vice president.

19. For more than a century Senators were elected by _____.

20. Prior to the _____ Amendment, a Negro was counted as three fifths of a person for the purpose of legislative apportionment and direct taxation.

Now check your answers on page 102.

Answers to sample Constitutional examination

1. second
2. 7, 25
3. 30, 7
4. vice president
5. tie
6. House, Senate
7. chief justice
8. state governor
9. state governor, writ of election
10. House
11. President, two thirds, Senate
12. President

13. *c*
14. *b*
15. *b*
16. *c*
17. *c*
18. *b*
19. *c*
20. *c*
21. *a*
22. *b*
23. *c*
24. *c*
25. *e*
26. *b*
27. *a*

The Bill of Rights
1. 2
2. 4
3. 6
4. 9
5. 7
6. 5
7. 10
8. 1
9. 3
10. 8
11. 5
12. 1

The Other Amendments
1. 19
2. 23
3. 11
4. 26
5. 17
6. 25
7. 13
8. 12
9. 18
10. 21
11. 24
12. 13
13. 20
14. 15
15. 14
16. 22
17. 16
18. Speaker of the House
19. their state legislatures
20. 13th

Glossary/Index

Antifederalists—Those who opposed ratification of the Constitution, 14

Armed forces, 2, 17, 32, 38, 56, 90–91, 94

Articles of Confederation—The written Constitution of the United States, 1780–1788, 86–97

Attainder, bill of—A legislative act pronouncing a person guilty (usually of treason) without benefit of trial and prescribing outlawry or death and attainment (dishonor and loss of all civil rights). Applied in England in the Middle Ages and in early modern times. Guarded against in Art. I (Secs. 9 and 10), 33, 35

Baker v *Carr*—The landmark one-man, one-vote decision of the Warren Court, 49, 75

Blacks, 9, 15, 75, 94; *see also* Slavery

Brown v *Board of Education of Topeka*—Reverberating Supreme Court decision outlawing segregation in public schools, 75

Canada, 79 96

Capitation tax—Literally, a tax on one's head. A tax fixed equally on each person. Art. I, Sec. 9 prohibited this type of tax, but this prohibition was erased by the 16th Amendment, permitting the income tax, 34

Cohen v *Virginia*, 72

Commerce clause (Art. I, Sec. 8, paragraph 3)—"The Congress shall have power. . . . To regulate Commerce with foreign Nations, and among the several States, and with the Indian Tribes;" . . . When combined with the implied powers inherent in the "necessary and proper clause," also in Art. I, Sec. 8, this clause has been construed by Congress to have given it virtually total control of transportation and business, 31

Construction
   Loose—The liberal or "easy" interpretation which insists that certain powers can properly be "implied" from other specified powers. John Marshall was a loose constructionist, 70–72, 74–75
   Strict—The interpretation which argues that only powers specifically delegated to the national government are allowable. States'

Construction—*Cont.*
   righters, such as George Wallace, are strict constructionists who cite the 10th Amendment, 33, 59, 76, 95

Corruption of blood—Mentioned in Art. III, Sec. 3. In English history, a bill of attainder also "attainted" members of the victim's family, 42

Double jeopardy—A person tried once and found not guilty of a crime would be placed in double jeopardy if he were again tried for the same crime in the same court. Forbidden by the 5th and 14th Amendments. Where the crime is an offense against a federal *and* a state law, however, he could be tried in both federal and state courts, 57, 60

Dred Scott v *Sandford*—The 1857 Supreme Court case which ruled that a slave is property. This contributed to a situation which brought on the Civil War, 73; *see also* Missouri Compromise

Due Process—The standard steps provided by law for a judicial proceeding which take into account the basic constitutional rights guaranteed every citizen brought before the bar of justice, 57, 60

Eminent domain—The right of a government to take private property. Also, the procedure by which this action is accomplished and proper payment established, 60

Engel v *Vitale*, 76

Enumerated powers—Those powers specifically authorized by the Constitution. For instance, the powers of the Congress are enumerated (Art. I, Sec. 8), 31; presidential powers are named (Art. II, Sec. 2), 38–39; judicial power is delegated (Art. III, Sec. 2), 41–42

Escobido v *Illinois*—A landmark decision proclaiming the right of arrested persons to be represented by counsel, 75

Ex post facto **law**—On Wednesday George J. Citizen is convicted for having fished on Monday in a section of the river that on Tuesday was declared off-limits for fishing by the city council. A law enacted and applied *after* an act has been committed, 33

103